Living a Life of Awareness

Living a Life of
AWARENESS

DON MIGUEL RUIZ JR.

Hierophant publishing

All quotes from don Miguel Ruiz and don Jose Ruiz are from the books,
The Four Agreements and *The Fifth Agreement,* published by Amber-
Allen Publishing.

Cover design by Adrian Morgan
Cover painting by Nicholas Wilton
Interior design by Jane Hagaman

Hierophant Publishing
8301 Broadway, Suite 219
San Antonio, TX 78209
888-800-4240
www.hierophantpublishing.com

If you are unable to order this book from your local
bookseller, you may order directly from the publisher.

Library of Congress Control Number: 2013950710

ISBN 978-1-938289-23-1
10 9 8 7 6 5 4 3
Printed on acid-free paper in Canada

Dedication

To all whom I love.

Contents

Introduction

> You know you're in love when you can't fall asleep because reality is finally better than your dreams.
>
> —Dr. Seuss

I believe the whole point of inner work is to enjoy life. For me, this means accepting myself for who I am unconditionally. When life is moving along effortlessly, my unconditional love for myself allows me to enjoy every moment of life in abundance. When life gets difficult, I don't just weather the obstacles; I greet the ups and downs of life's journey with unconditional love for myself and the people in my life by understanding that I am only truly alive in the present moment. As long as there is life, everything is possible.

Truth is the moment when unconditional love blossoms in our hearts. The expression "I am worthy of my own love despite this hardship" is the seed that brings light into the darkest moment of our lives. Our conscious relationship with ourselves allows us to decide what is true for us in each moment.

The present, right now, is the only opportunity we have to make change. The past no longer exists. The decisions and choices we've made have brought us here, and they cannot be changed. We can think of all the what ifs, should bes, and could haves, but that won't change a thing. Likewise, the future does not exist. The consequences of the actions we take today will not come about for some time, meaning our future is completely wide open; anything can happen. The only thing we are able to control is this very moment, right now, where our choices and decisions make an impact upon our present.

Ask yourself: Am I making these moment-to-moment choices and decisions with awareness? Am I accepting myself unconditionally in the moment? Am I controlling my yeses and nos? Can I see the possible consequences of the choices I make? If my decisions are automatic, am I aware that I have a choice between a self-projected illusion and the truth presented in a moment of clarity?

In the novel *The Ingenious Gentleman Don Quixote of La Mancha* by Miguel de Cervantes, the delusional Don Quixote has a moment of clarity in which he sees a group of windmills in the distance as they truly are—*not evil giants,* but simply windmills. In that moment he can choose another path. But because Don Quixote prefers his illusions over the truth, he concocts a story to justify his continuous belief in the illusion.

This choice between truth and illusion doesn't occur only in novels. It presents itself continuously throughout life, moment by moment. In moments of clarity, every single one of us *consciously* expresses our choice. We can choose to continue to believe in giants, or we can see the windmills for what they are.

When we choose to believe in illusion over the truth, we lose sight of our *Authentic Self.* The illusion acts as a filter on all the information we perceive, and the decisions we make in the moment and the actions we take may not necessarily be true to us. On the other hand, if we are aware of and honor our truth, our choice will reflect that truth. At that instant, if we are willing to accept the truth, we have the opportunity for unconditional love. We know that our life is worth more than an idea.

Choosing to see things as they really are, and not just as we wish they would be, takes courage. It requires taking our ego, our judgments and preferences, out of the picture and accepting things as they are. The choice between illusion and truth is the same as choosing between conditional love and unconditional love. Conditional love is easier to give, in many ways. Conditions give us a way in and a way out; but it is ultimately untrue. Unconditional love, on the other hand, is more challenging but ultimately True with a capital *T*.

It is a matter of rejecting oneself or accepting oneself. If we see giants in the windmills, then like Don Quixote, the illusion is chosen. Maintaining the illusion then reigns supreme, trumping self and truth in the process. But if we choose to see the windmills, then we have accepted our truth unconditionally. This is the choice we make *every* moment of our lives.

If we see perfection through the eyes of our internal judge, who is always pushing us to adhere to some ideology or belief system, then perfection is conditional and based on illusion. We create and maintain illusions through our *agreements,* or the process of saying yes to certain ideas and no to others. For example, an agreement is formed every time we say something such as, "I will be happy when I lose some weight/have the perfect relationship/have X amount of money in the bank," and so on. Through our agreements we put this idea of perfection on a pedestal, not realizing that it's an illusion.

Once we have created this imaginary image of how we are supposed to be, we then judge ourselves for not living up to it. We look in the mirror and berate ourselves for our shortcomings. Then we do the same to everyone we know. We punish ourselves to shape us and motivate us to be perfect, because that is what we have learned through our domestication. We use the reward of acceptance for living up to an expectation.

Domestication, the system of reward and punishment, works like this: Every time you get something "right," you get a reward that makes you happy. Punishment comes when you do something "wrong." While *how* we are domesticated differs based on our family and our culture, the outcome is always the same: self-judgment and conditional love.

For example, let's imagine that as a child you were told that not eating everything on your plate was "wrong," or even a "sin." As an adult, if you do not finish a plate of food, your internal voice of self-judgment will come back loudly, and you will eat to avoid guilt rather than to satisfy hunger. There is no one to blame for this; it is the current human condition that has existed for generations. The point is to become free of it through awareness.

Perfection through the eyes of unconditional love is being aware that the only truth is this very moment, now. Everything that exists right now is perfect simply because it exists, because it is alive. Life is a masterpiece of art that is constantly transforming and evolving. Therefore, what is truth at this very moment can and likely will change. If it is something negative, we have the capacity to change it if we so desire, although it is not a condition of our self-acceptance. In accepting ourselves unconditionally, we accept our good qualities as well as the "flaws"—it is all valid and perfect.

What does perfection have to do with living a life of awareness? In manifesting our life, we can either see it as a continuously evolving masterpiece or as a flawed construction that must be fixed and molded to fit our *idea* of perfection. When we live a life of awareness, we see that perfection already exists. Rather than being flawed, a full life is simply a matter of continuing to do what we love to do and improving our skills or craft. We do this not because we are searching for perfection, but because perfection is expressed through the action of being alive. Practice makes the master. Life gets better and better not because it is "supposed to," but because it is the consequence of passion and unconditional love.

When our false ideas of perfection control us—in other words, when we are not living a life of awareness—our choice between yes and no is compromised. For every yes we give, we create and manifest something. For every no, something will not be manifested. This is the way we control our intent, the force of energy that moves life. I am the force that moves this body; the force is me. I *am* intent. The same is true for you.

Living a life of awareness comes from knowing how to use this force of energy, how to manifest or *not* manifest, and whether we are going to apply conditional or unconditional love to do so.

Consider a toddler who is first learning to walk. He wishes to walk for the sake of walking and expresses his intent every time he tries.

When he falls, he may cry, but even in the middle of crying he still tries to do his best to stand up. Sometimes he might even laugh when he falls down. That child does not judge himself for "failing." He simply gets up and manifests his intent once again. And eventually, he succeeds. That's because the desire, the intent, is that strong. When we are this young, our desires are completely our own, based solely on the fact that we *want* to do something.

But what would happen if the child experienced self-judgment as a result of domestication? He may stop trying to walk completely, or his motivation may not be sincere anymore: "I'll walk so nobody will think badly of me and reject me." For many of us, the fear of rejection is often used as a motivator to push ourselves beyond the limits of our comfort. However, when we do this, we may not be manifesting the life we truly want for ourselves.

Manifesting with unconditional love is accepting the life force that is us. Unconditional love goes beyond accepting every belief. It is about accepting our capacity to have positive or negative beliefs. It is about the whole. We are each capable of doing both positive and negative things in our lives (and oftentimes, when life gets complicated, things are not clearly 100 percent good or bad—and here adjustments take a little more fine tuning). Accepting the whole is accepting the Authentic Self that is me, that is you.

We have a choice. Yes, we can accept the negativity in us; but we can also decide to make positive choices that make us feel good. It is our free will to express our preference in life. For example, let's say that in a moment of clarity we discovered that we felt it was OK to judge everyone. We see that this belief was based on the illusion of self-righteousness. But in this moment of clarity, we say, "I don't want to judge anymore." We look back on the past and see the many times we have judged, and we realize that we can't take those times back. But we can forgive ourselves now, and we can ask for forgiveness from others when that is appropriate, because we have truly changed our mind in that moment of clarity.

But after years and years of practicing a belief—in this case, judgment—it has become an almost automatic reaction. Holding on to a new, more positive point of view may not be so easy. If we want to manifest this change of heart and create a new practice, we become aware of the moment we give life to a judgment and be on the look out for the triggers that make us judge. Paying attention to ourselves and getting to know ourselves all over again leads to mastery of awareness in which, using the Toltec symbols, we go from being a victim to a hunter, then finally a warrior.

The victim mentality is where we have subjugated our will to our attachment to domestication—a belief. It is only when we become aware of that subjugation, in that moment of clarity, that we can express the choice to change it. And the best way to change it is to accept the truth. In the example of judgment, we accept that we had domesticated ourselves to the illusion of self-righteousness.

Next we become the hunter. The hunter looks for opportunities to practice this change in point of view. One way to do this is by paying attention and remembering the Fifth Agreement: "Be skeptical but learn to listen." Skepticism is the action of consciously withholding our yeses and nos and not making automatic decisions. This gives us an opportunity to listen and to perceive life as it is.

Skepticism allows us to spot those moments that something triggers us to react automatically without awareness. We ask, "What is it about this situation that makes me give away my awareness and the power of my expression of my free will?" In that moment, we become aware that these situations can come continuously, each and every moment—at school, at work, while listening to political discussions, or even just hearing someone else having a conversation. In those moments, a judgment comes up inside us based on our attachments to our beliefs.

Once we are able to identify when old habits and agreements are trying to skew our vision, the warrior steps in. The warrior is born the moment we declare a "war for independence." Once we are free from making decisions automatically, we can then express our free will by taking an action with complete awareness.

The key to lasting change is unconditional self-love. For example, if we make an agreement not to make judgments, we have two choices. The first is to use domestication not to make judgments. In other words, we say that perfection is *not* to make a judgment. Then, every time we do judge, we also self-judge ourselves for not being the model of perfection! This system of reward and punishment is simply replacing one program for another. We have now made the Toltec tools another form of domestication.

The second choice is acceptance. Through the eyes of unconditional love, we accept that we do judge. This acceptance allows us to free up the energy of pretending to be something we are not. Thus, we begin to become aware by paying attention. And when we recognize a trigger to judge, we have a moment of choice. We ask with awareness, "Do I choose to make a judgment here or do I choose *not* to make a judgment?" If we make a judgment, it is because we want to. If we don't make a judgment, it is because we don't want to. This is the true expression of what we want.

When we are living a life of awareness, we realize we have a choice. We are in control of our yeses and nos. It is not about whether we are going to accept ourselves based on the *correct* decision. On the contrary, we already accept ourselves with unconditional love. Our decision is clearly based on what we want as expressed through our yes or no. At that moment, the pattern is broken, and if we say no to judgment, then we have shifted the direction of our intent.

We call ourselves warriors in the Toltec tradition not just because we are in a war, but because warriors have the discipline of awareness, where practice makes the master. How do we practice? By being aware of our triggers, and when the moment comes, by making the choice that expresses our true desire in life.

The Four Agreements, created by my father, don Miguel Ruiz, are:

1. Be impeccable with your word.
2. Don't take anything personally.
3. Don't make assumptions.
4. Always do your best.

And my brother, don Jose Ruiz, contributed a Fifth Agreement later on, which I mentioned before:

5. Be skeptical but learn to listen.

Let's take the Second Agreement, "Don't take anything personally," as an example. After someone I love says something to me, I recognize the moment I take it personally. I accept that I tend to make it personal. I know what that feels like, and I have already made the choice to accept myself for who I am. I also choose to use this agreement to make a change. The moment is coming; I recognize it. It is about to happen. It is here.

I have a choice: I can take it personally or not take it personally.

If I look at it through the eyes of the judge, that choice looks like this: "I want to be good with the Five Agreements, so I am not going to take that personally—especially since I am the son of don Miguel Ruiz and the brother of don Jose Ruiz." If I succeed, then I accept myself. If I don't, I judge myself for not living up to the name don Miguel Ruiz Jr. But even if I succeed, in this case, the motivator was merely the reward of self-acceptance. There was a condition behind my choice.

On the other hand, making this choice from a place of unconditional love for both myself and my loved one, I simply choose not to take what was said personally for no rewards or gain, but just to express my true desire. I already love myself. I am free to make the choice of "Yes, I will take it personally" or "No, I won't take it personally." The agreement is not a condition, but an actual instrument that allows me to remember how I am going to use my intent. I am worthy of my own love, regardless of who my family is.

The art of living a life of awareness comes down to perfection and unconditional love. It is realizing that in every moment in our life, we have a choice. We can choose to see the world through the eyes of the judge, whose motivator is conditional love. Here I can create a hierarchy and multiple levels of "I am better and you are worse." Or we can choose to see the world through the eyes of unconditional love. When we do this, there is no hierarchy. Everyone lives life expressing their uniqueness, which is how they say yes or no, regardless of whether or not they are aware of it. Life is perfect because it is the truth that exists at this moment. That is their life.

We always have a choice. I can change things with just one choice. If I like the way something is going, I can keep on doing it. If I don't like it, I can change it. This is not because I *have to,* but because I *want to.*

What matters is your choice: Do you choose to live life with awareness? Do you see the windmills, or do you prefer the illusion of the giants? When illusion bursts, the heartbreak is enormous. Loss will always bring hurt, but what is it that we are mourning? For example, if we lose a loved one, are we going to miss that person for who he or she was or because of the illusion we projected onto that person and the meaning it brought to us?

Living a life of awareness takes work, which is why we call ourselves warriors in our Toltec tradition. The discipline required to become a master requires constant practice. It gets easier to keep a discipline with time. As a warrior, every moment becomes a choice to continuously be aware. The choices made at every moment are based on truth, because we are always watching it. The mastery is being aware that we are alive, free to make each and every choice that shapes our life.

The only way for this knowledge to come alive is by practicing it. You will never learn how to cook or experience new foods if you don't move away from the cookbook and get into the kitchen. The same is true for every book of knowledge—especially the sacred books from around the world. If you merely read them, they are just words on the page. The flavors and meaning only come to life when you choose to put those words to use. That is when a lesson comes alive—when it becomes truth for you in that moment because it is an experience in life.

That is the purpose of the daily meditations in this book, to help you put knowledge into practice and to experience this transformation for yourself. I ask that you do only one mediation per day; give yourself time to adequately reflect on each passage and implement the practice. Doing more than one in a day reduces their potency.

Simply put, living a life of awareness means making meaningful choices every moment of our lives. We can choose to live through the eyes of conditional love or through the eyes of unconditional love. Making this choice is what allows you to create your life as an ever-evolving masterpiece of art.

That is my wish for you.

Meditations

Letting Go of Perfection

My father said to me, "Miguel, when you understand that you are perfect just the way you are, you will see that everything is perfect just the way it is."

But it's not easy to just wake up one day, say you're perfect, and actually believe it. Making such a dramatic change in perspective requires desire and commitment. First, you leave behind any false ideals of perfection: You release your attachment to what you believe it means to be the perfect you, and you stop judging yourself for not meeting your own expectations, accepting yourself for who you are at this very moment. You begin by learning to love yourself and giving gratitude every morning for being alive.

Practice

Stop whatever you are doing right now and take this moment to love and honor yourself. You are perfect just the way you are, because you are alive in this moment.

Began Nov. 14, 2018

Quieting the Mind

In the Toltec tradition we have a concept we call *mitote,* which represents the thousand voices that occupy the mind, all of which are vying for our attention.

Some narrators may speak from distortion, while others may speak from truth. The loudest ones usually manifest in the form of an attachment. Reason helps us tell the difference between the two, but if we become attached, it can be difficult to distinguish the truthful voices from the distorted ones. Depending on which narrators we are attracted to, we will perceive the world through their narration, thus creating our world in their image.

With awareness, we realize there is a deep silence that exists behind all of those voices, in that space between thoughts. One way to quiet the mind is to listen to that silence. If we look at our reflection and into our eyes, we will see what lies beyond them; we will see the truth.

There is no need to chase love, because we are love. Turn off the volume on your narrators, the voice of our knowledge, and simply engage the present. Release your attachment to what you expect to see, so you can see beyond it. At that point, the true image of love will appear.

Practice

Take the next few moments to quiet your mind by listening to the silence deep within you. When the mind is quiet, see yourself and others as pure love.

Choosing Happiness for Today

You've probably heard the saying, "Life's about the journey, not the destination." Yet many of us are waiting for some goal to be reached, some status to be attained before we can begin enjoying our lives. We say things to ourselves like, "I will be happy when I get this job/accumulate this amount of money/have this relationship."

There is nothing wrong with wanting to attain or achieve certain things, but if we make our happiness conditional on reaching certain destination points, our life will become a series of goals to obtain, with each one failing to deliver the promise of happiness we envisioned. Living this way means missing out on the beauty of the journey, the one that is happening right now.

Happiness can only be found in the present moment, not at some imaginary place in the future.

Practice

With awareness, notice when you attach to the idea of happiness in the future. When this happens, say to yourself, "I won't wait for happiness. I choose to be happy now."

Practicing Nonattachment

It's often said in spiritual circles, "Don't be attached to things." But in reality, we're often not attached to the thing itself but to the *idea* of that thing. We have a compulsive belief that we must acquire something outside ourselves to make us complete.

Any time you hear yourself say, "I need this" or "I need that," you know you are attached to that idea. You have made your happiness and self-love conditional on the acquisition of that thing.

Practice

With awareness today, remember that you need nothing outside yourself to be complete. You are already complete and perfect exactly the way you are at this moment.

Accepting Yourself as You Are

Society sends the message that to be somebody in the world, you need to go to the right school, get the right job, buy the right car, live in the right neighborhood, and so on. Only then will you be accepted; only then will you be somebody in the world.

This implies that right now you are nobody. Nothing could be further from the truth. The entire power of the universe resides in your very being. You are made of light and stars. There is nothing you need to do, nothing you need to acquire, as you are already perfect exactly the way you are.

Practice

Today, with awareness, notice when you're seeking fulfillment through something outside yourself. When this occurs, gently remind yourself that there is nothing outside you that can complete you, because you are already complete. At that moment, say to yourself, "I love you."

The Authentic Self

The Authentic Self is a term that describes the living being that has the capacity to engage life. Our Authentic Self is always with us; we simply have filters that can sometimes block our awareness of it.

Practice

With awareness, remember today that the Authentic Self is the living being that gives life to your body, enabling you to perceive and project life and interact with the Dream of the Planet. It is the energy that moves you. It is pure, unlimited potential. You are the Authentic Self.

The Dream of the Planet Starts with You

In the Toltec Tradition, we have the concepts of the Personal Dream and the Dream of the Planet.

The Personal Dream refers to how you see the world and how you in turn project the world. It all relates to your point of view. You are 100 percent responsible for your Personal Dream.

The Dream of the Planet is the relationship between two or more Personal Dreams. For example, if you and I were physically in the same space, and if you were to touch your fingertip to mine, I would say that 50 percent of our relationship ends at that meeting point. I am responsible for myself from my body through the ends of my fingertips—completely responsible—just are you are responsible for yourself through the tips of your fingers. When we meet, we'll experience synergy, and we all contribute our Personal Dreams to the Dream of the Planet. Ultimately, the Personal Dream is the more important one, for two reasons: that is where it all starts, and that is the dream you have ultimate control over.

Practice

Remember, if you want to change the world, the first step is *accepting yourself as you are in this moment,* and change, with the freedom that life gives you, if you want to. Awareness, or the practice of being in communion with this moment and my present environment, is the key.

Living Your Life as a Work of Art

The word *Toltec* means "artist" in English, and life is the canvas for a Toltec's art. I am aware that knowledge is an instrument by which I am able to interact with the world, and my yeses and nos are the chisels or paintbrushes with which I create. I engage in the Toltec tradition by choice, fully aware that the name Toltec refers to an action or agreement belonging to a philosophy.

Not calling myself a Toltec wouldn't lessen my agreement or the lessons I learn from this oral tradition. This means my agreement is not subjugated to an identity. I am free to choose to agree, disagree, scrutinize, and engage with the Toltec philosophy, or any other, as much as I want. I am free to relate and engage in relationships with people who have a preference for another tradition or philosophy.

This is true for every one of my beliefs: I engage it for as long as I want to, knowing full well that I am a living being with the full potential to experience life with or without that agreement. This is what gives power to my agreements; I make them because I want to. This is my art, my agreement: to allow myself to experience life in its ever-changing truth with love.

Practice

Today, remember that your beliefs exist only because you exist. Therefore, no belief is greater or more important than you are. This is true for every human being.

Identity

In the Dream of the Planet, everyone adopts a name and an identity to go along with that name.

Your identity can be based on things like the color of your skin, the nationality of your family, the religion you practice, the work you do, and the activities and hobbies you love to participate in. In this way, your name and identity give you a purpose, a sense of belonging. They are symbols that are useful tools when communicating with one another.

But remember to never confuse any of these identities you have adopted with who you really are. These identities are simply symbols you play with that allow you to participate in our collective Dream of the Planet. You lose awareness the moment you confuse these identities with who you really are, and suffering is the result as it leads to our domestication based on these symbols.

Practice

Think of the people you know and the identities either they have assumed or you have ascribed to them. What identities have you adopted for yourself? How do you portray those identities in the world? With awareness today, remember that any identity you adopt is not the real you. Who you really are is far, far greater than can be contained in any identity or role. A particular role may die or dissolve, but you will remain.

Who am I?

Fear and Attachment

I know that whenever the fear of change takes hold of me, it means I have created an attachment to something outside myself. In change, the world I know can disappear, forcing me to go into the uncomfortable darkness of not knowing.

But change is inevitable, and it arises time and time again throughout our lives: a relationship ends, we lose a job, leave a home, get a new wrinkle, a graying hair, or experience the death of a loved one.

If you look at all the things and ideas you have become attached to, you will find that your identity is entwined in these attachments. Fear comes when these attachments are threatened in some way, because you have interpreted these attachments as being an inherent part of yourself, when they are actually arbitrary and ephemeral.

Practice

With awareness, notice how every time you cling to an object or an idea, you are in essence defending your definition of self. Release this attachment by remembering you are far greater than any object or idea you ever encounter. Let it go with ease and grace.

Examining Your
Uncomfortable Emotions

Your emotions—regardless of the triggers—are expression of yourself. Uncomfortable emotions let you know there is a problem to attend to, a wound for you to work on, thus allowing you to see your own truth. With awareness, you can observe your uncomfortable emotions, as they may be showing you a belief that you are holding which is no longer true for you.

Whenever an emotion is triggered, it is the opportune time to ask questions such as:

- ❖ What is this about?
- ❖ What agreement is at the heart of this?
- ❖ What attachment does this threaten?
- ❖ Do I really believe this?
- ❖ Is it important?

Answering these questions gives you the opportunity to examine your beliefs and determine which ones are still true for you today.

Practice

A feeling of anger, anxiety, or fear is often an indicator that something is out of line between your attached beliefs and your inner
truth. Next time you're feeling stressed, take a moment to ask
yourself the series of questions above. If your response is out of
step with what you think you believe, you know you've uncovered
an outdated belief.

Believing Your Own Stories

In the introduction, I mentioned *Don Quixote,* one of the greatest literary masterpieces to emerge from the Spanish Golden Age. The protagonist of the story, a retired gentleman named Alonso Quijano, becomes so caught up in books about chivalry that his perception of reality becomes gravely distorted, and he transforms into someone else: Don Quixote. Don Quixote sees the world through the filters of fantasy and adventure. Whatever reality presents itself, he redirects the story to fit his own expectations and beliefs. Maintaining the illusion becomes paramount—more important even than his sanity.

Without awareness, we all behave like Don Quixote, trying to change reality to fit what we believe to be true.

Practice

Notice when you are constantly investing in the stories you want to believe. Whenever your story does not match your beliefs, you judge it as imperfect. In addition, notice how you punish yourself for not living up to your own imaginary story. When you see this cycle for what it is, leaving it behind becomes much easier. You are perfect just the way you are, no story needed.

Freeing Yourself
from Domestication

Domestication, the system of reward and punishment, works like this: Every time you get something "right," you get a reward that makes you happy. Punishment comes when you do something "wrong." While the ways we are domesticated are different based on the individual and culture, the outcome is always the same: self-judgment and conditional love.

For example, let's imagine that as a child, you were told that not eating everything on your plate was "wrong," or even "a sin." Then years later, as an adult, if you do not finish a plate of food, your internal voice of self-judgment will come back loudly, and you will eat to avoid guilt rather than to satisfy hunger.

There is no one to blame for this, it is the current human condition that has existed for generations. The point is to become free of it.

Practice

With awareness, strive to recognize the ways in which you have been domesticated. When you see the domestication, be the Toltec warrior, saying to yourself, "I am now aware of this, and I choose to be free."

Recognizing What Matters

The beautiful thing about realizing our own mortality is that it puts the relationships we have with others and ourselves into perspective. In this light, any resentment we may be carrying toward another or ourselves is a type of early death. It has often been said that "holding on to a resentment is liking taking a poison pill and waiting for the other person to die."

Don't waste time letting a wedge come between you and those you care about when you have this present moment to share with one another. Forgiveness is the key to experiencing love and joy in the present moment.

Practice

With awareness, forgive yourself and others for any wrongdoings, real or perceived. In the big picture of life and death, does any resentment you are holding on to really matter?

Intimate Relationships

While we don't generally voice these statements aloud, many of us approach our intimate relationships in the following ways: "I will love you if you behave in a certain way. I will love you if you love me back. I will love you if you do what I ask and make me feel good about myself. And, of course, I will shun you if you don't."

When we bring this attitude into any relationship, what we are really attempting to do is to use conditional love to control the other person, to domesticate them to our own point of view. The eventual result of this is our own suffering, as feeling good at the expense of another is never genuine or sustainable.

Here is an example of unconditional love: I have a friend whose wife left him for another man. He loved her dearly and was very saddened. When I asked him how he was holding up, he explained to me that while he was upset, if being with another man made his wife happier than being with him, then that is what he wanted for her. As for himself, he wanted to move on with his life and enjoy a relationship with somebody who loved him as he loved himself. He was no longer living in an illusion, and he was grateful for that.

Practice

With awareness today, look for examples in the world of how uncon-ditional love is not determined by another's behavior. In which of your relationships are you loving yourself and others uncondition-ally? In which relationships are you living in an illusion?

I love you just
The way you
are,

Finding the Origin
of Your Agreements

Self-judgment is the punishment you give yourself when you fail to meet your own expectations, when you fall short of what you think you are supposed to be. You judge yourself for not living up to a self-imposed standard, to a belief. But any faulty belief that you have about yourself didn't originate with you; it came from someplace else, and you agreed with it.

So the next questions are: Where did you learn it? From whom? And why? The purpose of this questioning is not to place blame on anyone else, but rather to realize the moment when you said yes to this belief, so that you can discard that belief anytime you want to change your intent and be free from it.

Practice

With awareness today, hunt for your self-judgments. When they arise, examine where they came from, then discard them. Remember that you are perfect in this moment because you are alive, and you choose how you want to express your intent. Be free to love yourself.

Keeping Knowledge in Perspective

Knowledge serves an important purpose in the Dream of the Planet. It allows us to communicate with one another from a place of shared experience. It also allows us to go beyond our physical limits and use technology to live more comfortable lives.

Without awareness, knowledge can take over the mind. Everything that comes into your field of awareness could be constantly labeled and translated based on past experience. Knowledge also enables domestication, a system of reward and punishment that offers your own self-acceptance and the acceptance of others in exchange for conformity.

This is why the question "Are you using knowledge, or is knowledge using you?" is so important. You are primary, and knowledge is secondary. Is your mind so overrun by what you know that you have forgotten this central piece?

Practice

With awareness today, remember that knowledge exists only because you do. While knowledge can change, the presence that you are does not change. Remembering this helps you from becoming stuck in your beliefs.

Seeing beyond Your Filters to Discover Your Personal Dream

No one else will ever know what it is like to live life through your point of view. . . . You are the only one who knows how wonderful it is to feel that pleasure of eating a meal you enjoy, of hugging or kissing someone, of simply being alive. . . . This is your Personal Dream. You can make it the most beautiful paradise or the most perfect nightmare; it is all based on what you believe in, what you think, what you know.

—*THE FIVE LEVELS OF ATTACHMENT*

Seeing beyond our filters—our accumulated knowledge and beliefs—does not always come naturally. We have spent years growing attached to our worldview, and it feels safe. Whatever we become attached to can begin to shape our future experiences and limit our perception of what exists outside our vocabulary. Like blinders on a horse, our attached beliefs limit our vision, and this in turn limits our perceived direction in life. The stronger our level of attachment, the less we can see. If my attachment to "what I know" blinds me to all the available options, then my knowledge is controlling me; it is controlling my intention, and it is creating my Personal Dream for me.

Practice

Today, become aware of the beliefs to which you are attached; allow yourself to become free of them and to live as you choose.

Staying Flexible in Your Plans

While it's often a good idea to have a plan for what you want in life, it's equally important to remember that plans can change.

The one thing we can be sure of is that in our journey through life things will arise and try to throw us off balance, making our original road tough to follow. Often life goes in a direction we couldn't have imagined. The question then becomes, how do we react when this happens? Are we open to seeing that life had better plans for us than we did? Or do we lament the past, thinking that things could have been better *if only* this or that had not occurred?

Part of enjoying the life we have now is giving up the idea of what we thought we wanted in the past, because we no longer want it.

Practice

With awareness today, look at any remaining stories you have about what "could have been" in your life. If you don't have any lingering stories or regrets, that's wonderful. If you do, I invite you to release them, because the life you have right now is the perfect one for you.

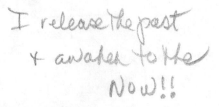

I release the past
+ awaken to the
Now!!

The Narrators

Part of the human experience is that we are constantly describing, classifying, and judging in our mind everything we experience in the world. This is what my father referred to as the "voice of knowledge." I call this internal chatter the "narrators."

The narrators talk about whatever catches your attention, and they describe things through the lens of your existing beliefs. These voices are constantly telling us how we should think about or react to any situation. They can keep us rooted to past experiences as we try to make sense of the present. They have a predilection for fitting new experiences neatly into our preconceptions of life.

This habit is self-limiting, because constantly fitting every experience you have into the box of what you already know keeps you from learning something new. Ultimately, you will be pulled out of awareness and away from your experience of the present moment in favor of locking in a comparison to the past.

Practice

If you are unaware, your narrators will run your life by making all your decisions automatically, based solely on your past experience and your existing beliefs. Remember that while your narrators may talk and talk, they are not who you are, and, consequently, you don't have to agree with them. Awareness is key in distinguishing the narrators from the true voice of your Authentic Self.

Surrender

In the Dream of the Planet, the word "surrender" has a negative connotation. It is often thought of as a weakness or deficiency, the final act of a "loser." But in my dream, surrender has the opposite meaning.

Surrender is the art of letting go, of giving up the ideas of what "should" and "should not" be. It is no longer fighting the rain.

But to surrender does not mean you become a doormat. In surrendering, you're not going to start allowing others to walk all over you. Your intent, your yes and your no, is still strong. Rather, to surrender means that as you move through life, you change the things you can and don't worry about the things you can't.

Practice

Have you surrendered today? With awareness, say to yourself: "I am no longer attached to the outcome of any situation, because life knows better than me." Embrace things as they are, not as you think they "should" be.

Following Your Heart

Beliefs don't have an independent existence; they are not "out there" in the universe somewhere, but rather reside only in our minds. We give beliefs power the moment we agree with them, when we say to ourselves, "This is true." But since we are ever-changing beings, our beliefs will necessarily change, too.

When we try to hold on to beliefs that no longer serve us, the result is suffering.

Trying to hold on to old beliefs just because they're familiar is easy to do; we prefer the known to the unknown; the status quo that's OK to the new adventure that might fail. But following your heart will never lead you astray. The war can be over anytime you want.

Practice

The next time you find yourself struggling, look at the belief you're trying to hold on to and ask yourself: Do I really believe this? Is holding this belief making me happy? Does it feel true to me?

Taking the time to identify these points of discord will help you shape the way forward, making sure your actions are in line with what you believe in the here and now.

Harnessing Intent

In the Toltec tradition, we define *intent* as the basic energy that exists, the life force that produces everything in the universe.

While intent is similar to what we normally call *intention,* it's not quite the same, because intent is bigger than intention; it is the power behind intention. Imagine that intent is like a wave, and intention is the surfboard on which we ride the wave.

Although we can't control intent, we can harness its power. That's why our thoughts, our words, and our beliefs are so important. Our greatest gift as humans is that we are able to create—we can create great cities, works of art, fabulous literature, and, most important, a life of love and peace (or pain and suffering—it's our choice).

This power exists within you. When you imagine something, you have the capacity to make it so.

Practice

What are you imagining today? You have the power to make it so. Next time you want something to happen that seems out of reach, imagine the wave of intent propelling you forward. Grab a surfboard and ride. Make your imagined goal become real.

Passion

Passion is a beautiful thing. It is the motivator by which we can realize our dreams. But the fear of failure can create such a strong vision that it will paralyze our intent and extinguish the flame that fuels the passion. Simply put, fear can keep us from living the life of our dreams.

One way to overcome this fear is to question it by asking yourself things such as:

- ❖ What am I afraid of?
- ❖ Where does this fear come from?
- ❖ Am I willing to let fear keep me from pursuing my passion?

Focusing on all the steps it may take to achieve your final goal can have the effect of fanning the flames of fear. Instead, just take one small step forward in the direction of your passion. With this step, you become aware of the strength of your intent, and the fear begins to fade away. Once you've taken several steps, you're on your way to manifesting your dream, and your accomplishments will reinforce your trust in yourself.

Practice

With awareness, become aware of the fears that are keeping you from pursuing your passion. Instead of focusing on the fear, just focus on taking the first step toward your goal. You don't need to consider all the steps necessary to fulfill your dream just yet—that will come with time. After this first step, your intent will take over.

Remember, you are powerful beyond your wildest dreams.

Rediscovering the Authentic Self

The Authentic Self is always present, and it is only our attachments that keep us from remembering who we really are. . . .

When we were born, our parents lifted us up and held us in their arms. They envisioned endless possibilities for us in their love for us. They saw the unlimited potential of our Authentic Self—the life force that could take any action in any direction that would lead to those possibilities.

—*THE FIVE LEVELS OF ATTACHMENT*

Practicing awareness takes discipline, a strengthening of our will that allows us to remain in a state of harmony with the world around us. Many religious and spiritual traditions in the world have created a discipline that fosters this harmony, such as prayer, meditation, yoga, chanting, and dancing, among many others. This knowledge is an instrument of transformation, and experiencing it is the manifestation of the Authentic Self.

I used to think that the world's greatest masters of every tradition were the best examples of the Authentic Self. Now I realize that everyone I know and see is a personification of the Authentic Self. We are all creating, producing, learning, engaging, and loving life. We are all the personification of life; we are always the Authentic Self. We simply make the choice to see it in ourselves and others.

Practice

With awareness, remember that every person you see is a manifestation of the Authentic Self. Say to yourself: "Today, I choose to see the Authentic Self in me, and the Authentic Self in you. Today, I choose to see the Realized Master in me, and the Realized Master in you."

The Parasite and the Ally

In the Toltec tradition, we sometimes use the terms "parasite" and "ally" when discussing the nature of the mind.

The parasite represents a mind that has been consumed by a relationship of simultaneous imposition and subjugation. Imagine a judge and victim, symbols that represent love based on conditions and domestication. The judge enforces the laws on which you've modeled yourself by dictating your worthiness for your own love, while the victim, subjugated by the judge, distorts all of its perceptions to satisfy the judge's view. This codependent and dysfunctional relationship forms the parasitic nature of the mind.

The ally represents a mind that has not been subjected to the conditional love of the parasite and is willing to perceive the world through an undistorted point of view. It is called the ally because it gives us the information we need to live with awareness.

When I see the world through the eyes of the parasite, there is disharmony in my life. If the ally is speaking, there is harmony. Both the parasite and the ally exist within me, and you, as reflections of the mind that reflect the whole. Loving yourself unconditionally means accepting yourself as having both.

Practice

With awareness, you can choose how you want to live your life. You can choose to live through the eyes of the parasite or the ally. That choice is an expression of your free will.

Making Changes
from a Place of Self-Love

The only motivation that brings lasting change is self-love. When you love and accept yourself, you want to treat yourself well and be as healthy as you can be. Only then do you have the freedom to detoxify from whatever has been subjugating your will.

When it comes to being motivated by self-love to make changes in your life, remove the "I musts" or "I shoulds" from your vocabulary. The key phrase is always "I want to make this change for me."

Making a change for yourself rather than to please others or to please your inner narrator makes all the difference between creating a temporary solution versus a lasting change.

Practice

What changes do you want to make for yourself today? Remember to make them from a place of self-love.

Co-creating the Dream
of the Planet

In the end, it is all about seeing knowledge as the building block to co-create a dream with another person while maintaining our awareness of self. I enjoy interacting with the Dream of the Planet. I enjoy using knowledge to communicate my dream with you. I enjoy playing with the world that surrounds me with respect and love. I am a part of this creation.

We can all become aware that it is love that bonds us to one another. We can love one another with conditions or with respect. The difference is harmony—a form of heaven on earth. When we have respect for one another's free will, then we have peace.

Practice

Today, show respect for others by honoring their choices, even when you do not agree with them. Show respect for yourself as well, by making choices with awareness and honoring your true intentions.

A Beautiful Dream

Imagine that you like soccer, and you suddenly find yourself at a stadium in the midst of a game in progress. It could be a magnificent stadium or bleachers next to a field. The players could be great or mediocre. It doesn't matter who is playing. You are not rooting for or against a side; you simply sit, watch, and enjoy the game for what it is.

The moment the referee blows the whistle to end the game—no matter which side has won or lost—you leave the game behind. You walk out of the stadium and continue on with your life. The game doesn't say anything about who you are. You are unattached, unaffected by the outcome.

Now imagine bringing that sense of nonattachment into your workplace, your personal pursuits, and your relationships. What would your life be like then?

Practice

With awareness, engage your life today with a playful sense of detachment. From this state of mind, you enjoy the things you do, but you are no longer attached to the outcome of any situation, as your identity is not contingent upon outdated ideas of "failure" and "success."

Setting Goals

While goal setting can be a good thing, it can also be used as a tool for self-domestication.

For example, oftentimes we create goals to validate ourselves as acceptable or unacceptable. If we achieve the goal, we accept ourselves; if we do not, we judge ourselves as failures. In this way, we are misusing goals and creating unnecessary suffering for ourselves and those around us.

A goal is the focal point by which we set our intent towards manifesting the life we want to live, and life is the process of manifestation.

Practice

Next time you are setting a goal, ask yourself:

- ♦ What is my motivation for doing this? Is it something I really want to do for me, or am I doing this to please someone else?

- ♦ Am I attached to a particular outcome, or am I open to all possibilities?

When you set goals for yourself and from the mindset of unconditional self-love, any outcome is a successful one.

Making Heaven on Earth

What is hell?

By my definition, hell is believing all the negative thoughts about ourselves and others that arise in our minds. These thoughts blind us from seeing life as it is, including our true potential and the potential of others. This is the only hell I know of, and it exists within us.

The good news is that heaven is also within us.

The difference between heaven and hell is the difference between unconditional and conditional love. The demons depicted in my nightmares represent the stories I create about the world, and they are contingent upon conditional love: "I will love you *if* you behave the way I think you should," or "I will love this situation *if* it goes my way," and, finally, "I will love myself *if* I achieve this or that."

By remaining open to all possibilities, and loving without conditions or restraints, we release ourselves to embrace everything as heaven. We love without any catch or hitch; and by no longer looking for the better, more perfect thing, we've accepted things as they truly are.

With all of the freedom of life, I say yes to loving you and to loving me. What do you say?

Practice

When you love and accept everything unconditionally, including yourself, you walk out of hell. When you no longer believe in the distortion of conditional love, heaven reveals itself inside you.

With awareness, say to yourself: "Today I love life unconditionally, allowing me to see the perfection that all manifestation is in every moment. Accepting and loving myself exactly as I am in this moment is to love *all* of God's manifestation."

Telling Stories

Some people tell a story about you that you like, and you like them in return. We call these people "friends."

Others tell a story about you that you don't like, and you don't like them either. These are our "enemies."

In both cases, you have defined yourself based on the opinions of others. Your ego is strengthened and your sense of personal importance is affirmed by outside, ephemeral sources. This is a dangerous way to live.

For instance, when someone loves you, you use his or her story to tell yourself that you are worthy of love. When you meet someone who doesn't like you, you agree with that, too, and judge yourself accordingly.

Although one of the Four Agreements is "Don't take anything personally," without awareness, you take everything personally. Everyone has been guilty of this at some point. You assume that others' actions are somehow motivated with you in mind, when in reality you have no way of knowing the other person's intentions or circumstances. By defining who you are in someone else's terms, you give away your power to define yourself.

Practice

Without awareness, everything that happens is personal. We often think the advice "Don't take anything personally" applies to negative ideas only. This is certainly where it starts, but remember that we shouldn't take positive ideas personally, either. You are beautiful and perfect, regardless of whether anyone else tells you so. Truth does not need confirmation from anyone.

Getting Clear about the Two Kinds of Fear

There are two types of fear in the world: physical fear and irrational fear.

Physical fear is a natural reaction to a clear and present danger. It allows us to survive by fleeing, fighting, freezing, or finishing a resistance with a rush of adrenaline and a desire to live. It is only trying to keep us safe.

Irrational fear triggers that same physical reaction, but there is no actual physical danger present. The main causes of irrational fear come from making assumptions or projecting about some future event. Irrational fear abuses our bodies by putting us through unnecessary trauma.

Coming to peace with fear means understanding the difference between the two types. One is rational and helpful, the other irrational and unhelpful. One can save your life; the other can stop you from living life.

Practice

With awareness, you can spot irrational fear when it arises. Next time you feel anxious or judgmental, chances are you're dealing with irrational fear. With awareness, remember that the solution to overcoming this type of fear is unconditional self-love. You are perfect just the way you are, and you have nothing to be afraid of. Love yourself just because you are.

Remembering Our Choice

It's easy to blame the media, our culture, or our community for perpetuating unrealistic images of what it expects of us. But at the very core of these expectations, there is no one to blame; because a commercial, like self-judgment, has no power over us unless we agree with its message. It is only when we willingly attach ourselves to these images and distortions that our happiness is compromised.

We do not need to take the blame for these self-judgments. We can simply become aware that they have been developing in our lives since childhood through the process of domestication.

Once we are aware of our self-judgments, we can reclaim our freedom by choosing for ourselves to transcend the rewards and punishment model that has been imposed upon us and eventually arrive at a place of self-acceptance. We have a choice. That is our power.

Practice

How many of your ideas and beliefs about the world and yourself are results of domestication and outside influence? Do you assume things should be or look a certain way because that's what you've seen on TV or in your community, and it seems normal? With awareness, question those assumptions today. Ask yourself if things might be otherwise and if you could be happy without these rigid ideals of perfection.

Forgiveness

Domestication is a two-way street. Although another person may have used his or her words and actions to attempt to domesticate you, or even to cause you harm or pain, ultimately you said yes to the belief and allowed it to blossom in your mind.

Becoming aware of your responsibility for your half of a relationship is crucial—it's not just the other person's fault. Recognize that you have been using someone else's words or past actions to potentially cause both of you harm simply by saying yes. Others' words and actions have power to hurt you only with your permission, which you give when you choose to agree with them.

Practice

Forgiveness happens the moment you say no to carrying the pain of an agreement that isn't good for you. Say aloud or to yourself, "I forgive myself and all others for using their words and actions against me, and I vow not to hurt myself again."

The act of forgiveness, for yourself and for others, allows you to move forward in life.

Engaging in Relationships— Not Imposing

> The Dream of the Planet can be as small as a dream shared between just two individuals or it can be as large as a dream shared amongst everyone in existence—and anywhere in between.
>
> What constructs the Dream of the Planet? It starts with you and [me]. . . . This relationship between us, however small it may be, is the dream called *us*. It happens when we interact with one another and the ideas, concepts, and agreements flow between us.
>
> —*THE FIVE LEVELS OF ATTACHMENT*

The Dream of the Planet is constructed by that need to share and communicate with one another. We either engage in a relationship based on respect, or we impose our own beliefs and ideals on each other disrespectfully, subjugating others to fit the mold.

Practice

Look at the relationships you have today with those at work, at home, and, most important, with yourself. Are you engaging in these relationships based on respect? Or are you attempting to impose your beliefs on others?

With awareness, say to yourself: "Today I choose to engage in my personal relationships instead of impose."

Becoming Aware of Your Beliefs

Since we are the living beings who give life to our beliefs in the first place, we must remember to shift our confidence away from our beliefs and back to ourselves.

Rather than having confidence in what we know, we have confidence in who we are. Instead of defending or debating a belief with all our might, we look and listen to what is going on around us.

Questioning ourselves and being open to changing our minds about something does not mean that we must question the core of our being. With self-confidence, we can simply question our beliefs and the stories we've created to describe our being.

Practice

Today, become aware when you feel the need to defend a belief. Ask yourself:

- ◆ Where did I learn this belief?
- ◆ How is this belief affecting me?
- ◆ Am I using this belief well?
- ◆ Do I still need this belief?

Vow to release any belief that no longer serves you.

Taking Off the Mask

As adults, we still have the ability to play make-believe as we did when we were children—that is, we still have the ability to create a mask based on our knowledge of how to engage one another in a particular setting. But as adults, the mask becomes a way to adapt socially and relate to a group with whom we are interacting, and we have forgotten that it's just a mask. We think the mask *is* us!

—*THE FIVE LEVELS OF ATTACHMENT*

For many of us, our attachment to beliefs—both our own and others'—manifests as a mask we don't realize we can take off. This mask prevents us from interacting with others and the world in a healthy way, and it forces us to make decisions based not on what we really want, but on what our beliefs dictate. As we release these attachments, our reality changes, since we are no longer chained to our beliefs. We are then free to create the lives we truly want by making new agreements that align with our Authentic Self.

Practice

With awareness, notice the beliefs to which you have become attached, realizing that you can discard those that no longer serve you.

Letting Go
of What You Know

Every time you label something—a tree, a grocery store clerk, a "good" idea—you've created an image, an abstracted representation, of what that thing is rather than experiencing it directly. You stop seeing the unique expression of this tree or that individual person. Whenever you classify something as "good" or "bad," you stop looking at it with an open mind.

This type of thinking can cause you to see and treat people as objects or ideas rather than living, breathing human beings, and you subtly judge them accordingly. This is how knowledge, in the form of your own labels and filters, keeps you from seeing reality as it is now.

Practice

Imagine you are visiting Earth from another planet. Look through the eyes of someone seeing this world for the first time. Let go of everything you know and everything you think for today, and see with new eyes.

Understanding Symbols

Words are symbols, and they make communicating with one another very helpful. But we attach emotions and meanings to words that are unique to us; we may have a slightly different interpretation or perception of a word, or the meaning could be entirely different from one person to the next.

A simple example of this is the word "red." There can be subtle emotional attachments to this word, both good and bad. At school, red markups to your work could mean you answered a question incorrectly. If a business operates "in the red," that means it's losing money. A bull charges when it sees red. Roses are red, and it's the color most associated with love. In the 1950s, it was an insult in most circles in the United States to call someone a "red." Today, it is the color of the Republican Party: We might say, "That's a red state."

The color red is a simple example. But what about words such as "death," "divorce," "love," "God," "enlightenment," or "freedom"? When communicating with one another, words can trigger certain emotional responses that are quite unintentional. That's why my dad teaches, "I am responsible for what I say, but I am not responsible for what you hear."

Practice

When you're speaking with someone, you're sharing a line of communication. But depending on our own point of view, you might be intending to say something different from what the other person hears. Be cognizant of words as symbols, and notice any emotional attachments you may have to certain words. This reminds you to not manufacture stories and also to not take things personally.

The Smokey Mirror

In the Toltec tradition, we have a concept called the *Smokey Mirror,* which refers to the filter we all have when viewing reality. Seeing the world through a Smokey Mirror means that whatever we see is distorted by our own beliefs and ideas, or our preconditioned point of view.

When speaking to someone whose smoke is very thick, you're only reaching their belief system; the filter of what they know makes it difficult (if not nearly impossible) to get through to the actual person. Conversely, someone might have a filter that is very thin, which means you're able to speak directly to them. We call this heart-to-heart.

The key is to become aware of how clouded your own mirror is or how attached you are to your own point of view. Your mirror is the only one you can wipe clean.

Practice

With awareness, realize that everyone you come in contact with is viewing the world through his or her own belief system. When you argue with someone, it's because that person is doing or saying something that is in conflict with your own belief system. When you approach anyone with an argumentative attitude, you can now see how your mirror is the one clouded with smoke.

Listening to the Silence

When the mind is not quiet, when our attention feels like it is being pulled in a thousand different ways, stress and disharmony take over. At this point, we are trapped in the fog of mitote (the thousand voices that occupy the mind). This fog obscures the reflection of love and makes us think that love is something that needs to be gained, like the elusive carrot on a stick.

With awareness, we realize there is a deep silence that exists behind all of those voices. One way to quiet the mind is to listen to that silence. If we look at our reflection and into our eyes, we will see what lies beyond them; we will see the truth. The quieting of your mind helps you to experience this moment without distraction and keeps you in your power.

Practice

Today practice quieting the mind. Take a few moments to just sit and relax. Remove yourself from all the distractions of the day and just reflect. Allow yourself to hear the silence deep within.

Redefining Success

In the Dream of the Planet, "success" is often equated with the acquisition of money, status, or possessions.

In my dream, success has a very different meaning. Success is the natural consequence of doing something we love to do, something we are passionate about.

Pursuing our passions helps us to evolve; it pushes us beyond the boundaries of our present limitations. Passion is the fire in our hearts, and doing what we love brings joy to our life.

Becoming aware of what we are passionate about, and then doing that, is the key. When we pursue our passions, success is the natural consequence, because our love for life is being expressed at every moment.

Practice

What are you passionate about? With awareness, give yourself permission to do what you love to do today.

Embracing Change

Sometimes change comes in the blink of an eye. Our internal narrators may agree it is for the better, or think it's for the worse. But we cannot avoid change.

Of the many things will change over the course of your life, there is just one thing that will never change: awareness. The constant point of perception that you are is unchanging. In this world of polarities (we consider "up" in relation to "down," or "hot" in relation to "cold"), we can only recognize change because of this part of ourselves that does not change.

Loving life unconditionally means knowing that life can shift without warning, just as the wind changes direction, but the strength of our own intent allows us to not only adapt to whatever life brings but also to thrive in our new circumstances.

Practice

Be in the present moment, continuously flowing with life, remembering that *you* are the constant in every second. Every change that occurs is happening "for you" instead of "to you."

The First Agreement

> Be Impeccable with Your Word. The First Agreement is the most important one and also the most difficult one to honor. It is so important that with just this first agreement you will be able to transcend to the level of existence I call heaven on earth.
>
> —DON MIGUEL RUIZ, THE FOUR AGREEMENTS

When it comes to being impeccable with your word—my dad's First Agreement—it's important to understand the effect our words have on our own behavior. For instance, if we're putting ourselves down in our minds, if we're telling ourselves that we are ugly, not good enough, or unworthy, what effect will that have on our sense of self? With this kind of negative self-talk, it's no wonder we lose faith in our own abilities and our own divinity. We would never stand for this type of treatment from another, yet many of us inflict it upon ourselves regularly.

The wonderful news is that these things are not true—they can't possibly be true.

Practice

Your word is the bridge from which you create and navigate your Personal Dream as well as the Dream of the Planet. You are a beautiful, worthy, perfect creation of God. Any time you hear yourself say anything to the contrary, remember it is time to be impeccable with your word to yourself.

Self-Investment

When you overinvest yourself in a relationship, you give your power over to it. Instead of going with the ebb and flow of life, you fight any change to that relationship whatsoever. A relationship that may have felt safe suddenly feels scary when you focus on not losing it.

But the reality is that no one will be with you forever, except you.

When you keep your energy focused on having faith in you, you will maintain your power and well-being. Calling your investment back does not mean that you do not value or cherish the relationship; in fact, it's quite the opposite. You will actually find that you are able to be more loving and present with both yourself and those around you as you deepen your loving investment in yourself, because you have the freedom to respect each other's free will. That respect creates harmony between individuals who love one another.

Practice

With awareness, notice when you overinvest your energy in your relationships. Take a few conscious breaths and imagine that you are calling your energy back and returning it to yourself. With each exhale, imagine that you are releasing your attachment.

Keeping Others' Opinions in Perspective

Avoiding rejection at all costs is a very common practice in the Dream of the Planet. No one likes to feel excluded or lesser than. For instance, if someone says to you, "I'm not attracted to you," you have a choice about what to do with that knowledge. You can accept the truth and realize that that person's opinion has nothing to do with you and has everything to do with that person and his or her particular taste.

Or you can take that person's preference and use it against yourself to reinforce some negative belief you have about yourself: *That person is not attracted to me because I am overweight, I am too short, etc.* (Unfortunately, this is the more common reaction.) In this way, you end up valuing someone else's taste preference over your own; you convince yourself that you are not deserving of your own love or acceptance. The motivation to make improvements suddenly becomes conditional: *If I lose a few pounds, maybe he/she will like me better.*

Either way, you are making a choice. You can choose to let your self-acceptance be subjugated by another person's opinion, or you can choose to accept that this person has simply stated what is true for him or her, and that does not change who you are.

Practice

With awareness today, notice when you subjugate your self-love to another person's opinion. Remember, you can respect the opinion of others without agreeing with them. Say to yourself: "I am perfect in this very moment, and this is my truth."

The Breath

Every second you are doing something that is crucial to life: you breathe. Most of the time, you do this on autopilot, breathing without even realizing you are breathing. But when you bring your conscious awareness to your breath, every inhale and every exhale can be a blessing to your body. Each inhale allows your environment to nurture you, and with each exhale you nurture the environment around you. The breath is a constant flow of generosity and gratitude.

Practice

Ask yourself: "What would I like more of in my life today?"

Now, restate your answer using just two words. For example, maybe you want more self-love and peace in your life . . . or wisdom and creativity . . . or abundance and faith. . . . You get the idea.

Use these words as a mantra as you breathe consciously. Say the first word with every inhale and the second word with every exhale. With awareness, notice the results of conscious breathing.

Engagement

"Engagement" is the action of interacting with the focal point of our attention. We become involved, in the form of an attachment, with a thing, situation, person, or idea by investing a piece of ourselves in it.

An engagement produces suffering when we become so attached that we forget that who we are is different from the focal point of our attention. When we lose this awareness, we bestow our inner power on something outside ourselves, and we surrender our happiness to the stability of this outer situation.

In the Dream of the Planet, everything is in constant flux; nothing stays stable for very long. Like dance partners who flow with the melody and rhythm of life, our job is to engage things with ease, remembering that who we are is not contingent upon something outside ourselves.

Practice

With awareness, remember to enjoy the flow today.

Having Fun

I often tell people to "have fun" when we are saying our goodbyes, and sometimes I get a strange look or a remark such as, "I'm going to work! It's not supposed to be fun."

It reminds me of when I was a child, and my friends and I pretended to be grown-ups. We would each choose a role, such as a lawyer, a doctor, or a bus driver, and our faces quickly adapted to the role by getting very serious. After a few minutes, we would finish the game and our smiles would come back. Then we would say, "That was fun."

But somewhere in time, our smiles didn't come back. The game never ended, and, more important, we forgot we were playing. We all have responsibilities—work or school, chores, bills that need to be paid. Though these activities sometimes aren't the most fun, we're still spending time with the person who matters most in our life: ourselves.

We can choose to enjoy what we are doing or not, regardless of whether it is the most mundane or stressful job we have ever experienced. The choice is ours. I hope you choose fun!

Practice

How do you want to experience your time today? With awareness, make fun a part of your activities today.

Seeing Your Authentic Self

For many years, I have had the privilege of seeing my father work and share what he knows, and in that time there has been one constant request from many who have studied under him:

"Don Miguel! Can you help me find the real me?"

My father would look at the person with a compassionate smile and say, "You are right in front of me."

The reply would usually be some variation of, "No, no. That is not what I am trying to say. What I mean is, help me find the real me. My Authentic Self."

Without realizing it, the student has just asked my father to redomesticate their entire belief system into one in which they can accept and love themselves. This is what they believe the Authentic Self needs to emerge.

What these students don't realize is that the answer is much simpler than that. You are the Authentic Self always. You don't need to reprogram yourself—you just need to know that you are the programmer. Love and accept yourself completely. That is all. Once you do this, you will be able to see that you are beautiful, perfect, exactly as you are, and this has always been the case.

Practice

Simply notice today that you are perfect. You are the Authentic Self. There is nothing to search for, because you are already here.

Reimagining Death

In the Dream of the Planet, many people have a notion of death that involves fear, emptiness, and loss. But consider that on a deeper level, no one ever really leaves us. Modern science has shown that on an atomic level, there has never been any more or less energy in the world than there is right now. Energy is never lost; instead, it is constantly changing, reforming, and reshaping. Since we are pure life energy, the same principal is true: No part of us is ever lost; it just changes form.

The spiritual translation of this scientific truth can be heard in the following statement, which is shared by nearly every major religious tradition: Death is not the end.

Practice

With awareness, remember that while people may move outside the point of your physical perception, no one is ever truly gone. Their energy and spirit live on; the same is true for you.

Domestication Can Occur Where You Least Expect It

The Four Agreements—be impeccable with your word; don't take anything personally; don't make assumptions; and always do your best—are wonderful teachings that have changed the face of humanity. But despite our best efforts, when we go into the world and interact with others, sometimes we don't follow them.

Here's the trick: If you beat yourself up by saying things like, "I took that personally; I am a failure at this!" or "I have been living a spiritual life for years, and I am still not impeccable with my word—ugh!" you have now redomesticated yourself and turned the Four Agreements into the four conditions for your own self-acceptance.

We all strive to be better people, and we're all going to make some mistakes along the way. The important thing is to be generous and optimistic in your efforts. Domestication is a tough road to exit, but you have all the tools you need to do it.

Practice

Be gentle with yourself today. If you find yourself falling short of a chosen ideal, simply notice it and forgive yourself. Make the action of standing up again the expression of resetting your will by forgiving yourself, and refocus your intention by choosing what you want to manifest with intent.

Finding Peace

While our points of view may differ, we are all products of the same source. The only things that separate us are our attachment to our own point of view and the belief that others must share it. This is where we begin putting conditions on our love for one another, and this is the source of conflict.

When you love unconditionally, it doesn't matter if others agree with your beliefs. You let them be who they choose, because you know who you are and that allows you to respect all of creation. We have a word for this: It's called *peace*.

May peace be with you today.

Practice

Today, try to focus on loving others and their beliefs unconditionally—especially when they have opinions that may differ from your own. You know the feeling when someone listens and respects your perspective without judgment; extend that feeling of openness to others, and watch as peace enters.

Wishing

Wishing is a popular pastime in our culture. You can wish upon a star, cash in your three wishes from a genie, or make a wish before you blow out the candles.

When you look deeper, there are really only two types of wishes: those that function as pleas and those that serve as prayers.

When wishing is loaded with expectation, you've created an attachment to the outcome. In this way, wishing with this intention is really a plea from the mind.

When you wish without expectation, your intention is a simple desire for good, to move things in a positive direction. The focus is on the potential and the possibility of change. This type of wishing is a prayer from the heart.

This one little difference of expectation can change a wish from an ego-driven demand to an openhearted request. By letting go of expectations, we focus our intent on positive change while remembering that whatever outcome occurs will ultimately be the best one.

Practice

When you notice yourself wishing something were different, make your wish a prayer instead of a plea. Let go of your attachment to the outcome, and relax into the freedom of trusting the universe.

Taking Control Away from the Narrators

Have you ever noticed the repetitive nature of your internal narrators? They constantly tell the same stories, repeat the same judgments, and debate the rightness or wrongness of every thought you have and every action you take: "This is bad, that is good; do this, don't do that; etc."

When you lose awareness of your Authentic Self within these stories and comments, they begin to run your life. All your decisions and actions become automatic; you have effectively relinquished control of your thoughts to the internal narrators, and they're running free.

Practice

With awareness, begin questioning the voices of your internal narrators. Notice how they play the same tapes over and over again. Is it time for a change? This single act of just stopping to listen to your heart instead of your narrators will help you regain the power to make your own decisions consciously and deliberately.

Feel Your Emotions

While your emotions are genuine, and no one can say how you ought to feel, it's important to remember that what triggers those feelings may not always be real. Emotions are like a car alarm: They keep you present and are a beautiful way to uncover those little agreements, conditions, distortions, and wounds that your storytelling is trying to hide.

An emotional reaction is an invitation to remove something from hiding and reevaluate it. Rejecting your emotions is simply an attempt to cover up old wounds.

Practice

The next time you have an emotional reaction to something, rather than denying or attempting to cover up your emotions, say to yourself, "This is my truth, and now I am reacting to it." With that statement alone, you are no longer using your energy to deny the truth, but opening the door to healing and releasing instead.

The Two Types of Happiness

I often say that the point of all this work is to be happy and to enjoy life. But as I look around the Dream of the Planet, I see two types of happiness: real and illusory.

Real happiness is based on seeing the truth, and it occurs every time you accept the world as it is in this very moment. Illusory happiness is when you surround yourself with stories that are not true, then expend all your energy defending them to survive.

It's a huge difference, because if there's a story that needs defending, then you need to impose your will to enforce it. In other words, you need the people around you to believe it, too. Any time you're in a position of trying to exert your will onto someone else, you're in a fearful place.

Happiness based on truth is a life without irrational fear. You are happy to share with others, but you do not feel the need to domesticate them to your own point of view. You feel secure and confident, and at peace.

Practice

Things in the exterior world may crumble to the ground at any moment; this includes any stories. But when your faith is laid in your center, any exterior change does not affect the aware presence that you are. Your happiness is true. Remembering this gives you the ability to distinguish truth from illusion.

The Goals of the Ego

Our ego, or our sense of personal importance, is constantly trying to define itself to the world. It is fueled by a need to be right, to win, and to know everything. Any time you find yourself struggling, fighting, or arguing with others (and yourself), all in an effort to defend and maintain your beliefs and ideas, that is your cue that you have become attached to the goals of the ego, and now your ego is running your life. It is through these beliefs and ideas that the ego has constructed the story of "you"—so it's no wonder defending them elicits such an emotional reaction.

The ego builds itself on the belief that we are separate entities, disconnected from and in competition with one another. But nothing could be further from the truth. When you realize your interconnectedness to all beings, the ego can no longer control you. The function of the ego is to keep the illusion alive.

Practice

With awareness, notice when you feel compelled to dominate those around you, either by aggressive or passive-aggressive means. When this happens, your ego is controlling your life. Remember that you are not in competition with others; we are all connected, and no one deserves to be dominated—not you and not anyone in your life.

Questioning

Children are known for asking questions. "What is this?" "Who is that?" "Why do we do this?" But as we become adults, many of us question less and less, instead thinking that we "already know" the answers.

The mind that stops questioning also stops growing. In this way, questioning can be a good thing. When we question what we think we know, we begin to expand our awareness again.

Practice

When a belief comes into your mind today, ask yourself, "Is that true?" The act of questioning can produce a moment of clarity that allows you to see a new truth.

Blame

When you point fingers at others, two things occur. First, you get stuck in a mindset of blame and its counterpart, defensiveness. Blame is stuck energy, one that creates cyclical thinking as you justify your side of the story, your position, your "right" to feel like a victim. It might feel powerful in the short run to deflect some of the burden, but in the long run it is draining and nonproductive.

Second, you make other people responsible for your happiness. This isn't a responsibility most people want, and it's also not a reasonable thing to ask, anyway. Making your happiness contingent on the behavior of others is a dead-end road. What you are basically saying is, "When so-and-so changes, I'll feel better."

When you give up the habit of blame and take responsibility for your own actions, reactions, and responses, you are free to choose again with a fresh perspective. You will become lighter, shedding the old coat of blame, and step into the light of self-awareness and growth.

Practice

Imagine there is no longer any blame in your world; no finger-pointing and no judgment about what someone else should or should not have done. How would your perspective shift? What new actions would you take if blame were erased from your being?

With awareness, make today a blame-free day.

Perceiving Things as They Are

When we are living our lives from a place of awareness, we respond appropriately to any situation that arises. When we lose that sense of awareness, we get caught up in the "thousand things" happening all around us and the voices of our internal narrators; when life's challenges arise, we *react* instead of *respond.*

Being aware can be described as simply being in communion with the world around you, without knowledge filtering and distorting your perception of the world. Awareness allows you to perceive your surroundings just as they are, without the projection of your preconceptions, judgments, and illusions.

Practice

As you move through your day, remember to keep the center of your attention on the power within you. This will keep you grounded and calm. When challenges arise, you are now much more likely to respond than react.

Loving Unconditionally

Attachment is when you take hold of something outside yourself and confuse it with the power that resides inside you. When you fasten on to an idea or belief that something "must be" for you to be happy, you know you have attached yourself to it.

The strongest form of attachment occurs when you make the statement, consciously or unconsciously, that "this is necessary for me to love and accept myself." In so doing, you turn self-love into conditional love, because you have created an expectation that must now be met for you to be happy.

Practice

Remember today that the power of life is inside you, and you need nothing else to be complete. You are perfect just the way you are. Love yourself simply because you are.

Discovering Harmony

Every world religion and spiritual tradition has a name for the moment we become aware that nothing but harmony exists. In the Toltec tradition, we call this being in constant communion with our creator. The only thing that separates us from one another is our point of perception; together we make a whole.

Practice

Today, look at every person as an individual manifestation of the one whole life.

Noticing Your Words

"It's not fair!"

"Why me?"

"I don't deserve this."

Most of us have made statements like these at some point in our lives without realizing the impact they carry.

When you use these types of words and phrases, they will leave you feeling victimized and resentful. Instead of feeling like you have a choice in life, you now feel trapped and powerless. With this mindset, life becomes a struggle rather than a joy.

Through the practice of awareness, you realize that your choice of words has a big impact on how you see the world. By becoming aware of both the words in your head and the words on your lips, you can choose to use the words that serve you best.

Practice

The Toltec hunter learns to watch his or her word choices, releasing any statements that sabotage and drain energy. With awareness, notice the nonhelpful statements that give your power away. Remember, you always have a choice.

Dropping the Story

Perhaps you've played the game in which you watch people in a public place, restaurant, or other setting and make up stories about who they are, what they are doing, what their backstory could be. While this game can be amusing, the problem is that most of us live out a real-life version of this almost constantly: We all have an innate need to describe what is happening before us.

When we meet or interact with someone, we project a story onto him or her based on how we look at the world or what our particular belief system is. All of these little stories are ultimately assumptions, and they cloud our ability to see things as they truly are, free from our attachments.

Practice

When you see or interact with people today, become aware of the little assumptions you make about them. Notice how these judgments are habitual. Then try to simply watch people without any judgment or backstory. When a judgment or label comes, notice it for what it is, and remember that you don't have to believe it.

Truth versus Illusion

Whenever I'm upset, I know that something I hold to be true has been put to the test. I look at that agreement inside and out and ask myself: Is this an agreement based on truth or illusion? If I am attached to the agreement, I will use a lot of energy to keep it alive. But if I have to struggle that hard to give an idea or belief life, it cannot be very solid, can it?

The next time you feel like one of your opinions or values has been challenged, take a moment to identify what agreement you've made to support that idea. To maintain your opinion, do you need to ignore or defy other people's opinions or disregard new information that's come to light? Ask yourself how attached you are to your truths; you may be compromising the real truth to maintain your status quo.

Practice

With awareness, say to yourself: "As a Toltec hunter, I will notice when I start to struggle, so I may see the illusion I am trying to hold on to. Once recognized, I vow to let it go with ease and grace."

Transitions

What are the first things you think about when you open your eyes in the morning? What are the last things you think about before you go to sleep? In the Toltec tradition, we pay a lot of attention to the mind's transition from the waking dream state to the sleeping dream, because transitions are an excellent place to bring in more awareness and to come into more choice.

Are your early-morning and late-night thoughts pleasurable? Or does your mind cycle through worries, problems, and questions? Remember, you are not a helpless bystander to the tyranny of your mind. By becoming aware of your thoughts in the space before you transition, you can help to set the tone for your day and night.

Practice

Take a minute to reflect on what you woke up thinking about this morning. Remember that you are an artist. Are your thoughts the art you want to be starting and ending each day with? Before you go to bed tonight, fill yourself up with thoughts of what you are grateful for, what you love about your life, and what you are excited about for tomorrow.

Changing Your Tone

Our inner narrator is constantly interpreting the world, filtering our experiences and perceptions and pigeonholing them into what we already know.

This narrator can be either a parasite or an ally. For example, if I stand in front of the mirror and pay attention to my thoughts, I might hear something like this: "Miguel, you are fat, you look horrible, and you need to lose weight now!" In this way, my inner narrator is operating as a parasite, pushing the agenda of domestication and conditional love.

But if when I stand in front of the mirror I hear this: "Miguel, I love you very much, and you may want to lose some weight just to be healthy," then my inner narrator is functioning as my ally. I hear my thoughts without any judgments, without any justifications, and I say to myself, "This is me, and I love it."

Practice

Go stand in front of the mirror right now, look yourself in the eye, and say, "This is me, and I love it!"

Broadening Your Horizons

While life has every right to say no to our endeavors, too many times we say no to ourselves preemptively when we think things like, "I'm not good enough," "I can't do it," or "I'll never make it."

In this way, we are judging and rejecting ourselves before life has had a chance to express a choice. This self-rejection stops us from living the life of our dreams and keeps us trapped in disillusionment.

The way out is through unconditional self-love. Loving ourselves unconditionally gives us the opportunity to enjoy the greatest love of our life—ourselves. This type of love is not based on the false image of ego, but on truly accepting ourselves for who we are at this moment.

In this way, we respect ourselves by being willing to try new things. When life says no to us, as it inevitably will sometimes, we respect that choice also, without self-judgment. But who knows? Life might just say yes!

Practice

With awareness, don't be afraid to try something outside the normal boundaries you have set for yourself. Be optimistic, and always do your best. Life will take care of the rest.

Understanding Knowledge

Our mind has a need to name, describe, and understand the things that happen in our lives. We call the result of this process "knowledge," and it helps us to understand the world and the universe and to communicate our ideas with others as we co-create the Dream of the Planet. But when it comes to understanding ourselves, knowledge is of little use. You may say things like, "I am a doctor, a father, a husband, a student," but these words describe only the roles you play; they say nothing about who you really are because you are much more than just a symbol.

Practice

Ask yourself the most important question: "Who am I?"

In your response, remember: Who you are is not your job, your life role in relation to someone else, or a role you aspire to have. Rather, who you are is who you are at the center. The answer is beyond all knowledge and cannot be expressed in words. Meditate on this today.

Habits

Sometimes we have habits or practices that cause us pain, yet we continue to do them. This is because that same action also brings us comfort in some way. Being honest with ourselves in this regard is key to knowing whether or not we really want to change them.

When we look deeply and honestly at habits we can't seem to let go of, one of two things will occur: Either we will see how this habit is not benefitting us at the deepest levels, and we will be able to change that habit much more easily; or we may find that we are only trying to stop a habit or practice because we have been domesticated into thinking it's really bad, but that for ourselves, we don't really feel that way. In this case, our agreement is renewed, and our habit becomes a better word—a "practice."

In either case, awareness in the moment is key.

Practice

With awareness of how we really feel about a particular habit, we regain something very important: our ability to make a choice, to say yes or no all over again. Having unconditional love for yourself is the key to knowing what is really true for you.

Letting Go of Others' Expectations of Who You Should Be

Many of us have spent years creating stories about ourselves based on other people's ideas and expectations, then we struggle through life trying to live up to these false images that we agreed to.

But there comes a point when you say to yourself, "This is who I am—no story needed." At that moment, you see your inherent perfection, and this realization is all you need to enjoy life. From this new perspective, you can change your life in any direction you see fit, because you now have the freedom to choose. You have stopped trying to live up to someone else's beliefs and ideals.

As a result, you do not make changes in your life because you feel you must do so to love and accept yourself; rather, you make changes from a place of self-love, to express yourself and experience more of life, because you already know there is nothing you need to do, nothing you need to attain; you are perfect exactly as you are.

Practice

Remember to enjoy your perfection today. You are perfect; you are life.

Inner Listening

Taking some time for yourself every day is just as important as brushing your teeth or combing your hair. For you to be at your best, take the space and time to simply be, without deadlines, distractions, or interruptions. When you don't get enough time for yourself, irritability, tiredness, and even burnout can result.

Awareness takes presence, and presence takes inner listening. Inner listening is a learned skill that is most easily practiced in stillness. Once you have discovered the rhythm of inner listening, it becomes integrated into every moment, no matter how busy or loud.

Practice

Right now, close your eyes and take one minute to simply sit in stillness and listen to the silence within . . . and breathe.

Living in the Past

Your enjoyment of this present moment can easily be dragged down by the memories of the past. When you don't release the past, you drag it around with you. Everything you see is filtered by where you have been, rather than where you are now and where you want to go.

Some of the biggest burdens many people carry revolve around past relationships. For example, when you think about an ex-partner, is there a sense of spaciousness and ease, or does your belly tighten and your mind begin to race?

Releasing the past takes a willingness to let go of being right or being wronged. When you wave good-bye to what was with lightness and clarity, you are then in a better place to create a bright future.

Practice

Send a mental blessing to your ex-partner, ex-spouse, ex-boss, or ex-landlord. Think of all the things you are grateful for in that experience and let everything else go. With awareness, let this day be about forgiveness and gratitude.

Finding the Origin
of Your Self-Judgments

Every time we don't live up to our self-imposed conditions, our own measurements of "success," our internal judge says things like, "You have failed" or "You are not worthy."

Other individuals who have a need to impose conditions upon us often reinforce these judgments. The result of agreeing with them is that we deny ourselves unconditional self-love. With awareness, we realize that these judgments only have strength because we allow them to by believing them.

The good news is that it only requires a single step to begin to break free. As soon as we begin to question our beliefs, the walls of support that uphold our judgments begin to collapse.

Practice

Ask yourself:

- ◆ Where do my self-judgments come from?
- ◆ Why am I being so harsh with myself?
- ◆ Why would I choose to agree with someone else's sub-jugation of me?

Remember today that you are a perfect creation of the universe, and there is no one else in the world exactly like you! Love yourself exactly as you are.

The Second Agreement

Don't Take Anything Personally. Nothing other people do is because of you. It is because of themselves. All people live in their own dream, in their own mind; they are in a completely different world from the one we live in. When we take something personally, we make the assumption that they know what is in our world, and we try to impose our world on their world.

—DON MIGUEL RUIZ, THE FOUR AGREEMENTS

Many people have told me that of my father's Four Agreements, the second one, "Don't take anything personally," is the most difficult to practice.

One way to think about this is to understand that all people—me, you, and everyone else—uniquely perceive the world through our own senses, and, by definition, we can't possibly be having the same experience as someone else. We may dress similarly, we may speak the same language, but every single one of us has a different perception, and no two perspectives will ever be exactly the same.

Only in your imagination can you see the world through the eyes of another.

Practice

With awareness, realize it's impossible for anyone else to ever think or feel exactly the same way that you do, because to think and feel is by definition an individual experience. Consequently, you couldn't possibly know another individual's experience, because you are not that individual. Remembering this allows you to better practice not taking things personally, which allows us to be compassionate.

Respect

Regardless of how many lectures I might give to my children, they will learn respect by observing how I treat them, others, and, most important, myself.

Respect means that I honor the choices of another. I honor their yeses, and I honor their nos. Respect and unconditional love go hand in hand; you can't have one without the other. Like love, respect is contagious.

Practice

To teach love and respect to others is to practice it every moment. In every encounter you have with another person, ask yourself, "Am I showing this person respect?"

With awareness today, remember that your actions are your example to the world. Be the teacher of love and respect to all fellow beings by honoring them and their choices.

Breaking the Cycle
of Self-Flagellation

Many of us believe that perfection can be attained through hard work and dedication only. This belief is supported by many of the messages from the Dream of the Planet as well. While there's nothing wrong with striving to do better, as soon as our happiness and self-approval are hinged on achieving this perfection, we are endangering our own well-being.

From this point of view, if we do happen to achieve perfection for a moment, we reward ourselves with conditional self-love. Then we use this conditional self-love as our motivator to continue pursuing this distorted idea of perfection in the future. When we get tired or need to take a break, we judge ourselves harshly for doing so. It's a circuitous problem, and over time we lose perspective, and our efforts become counterproductive.

Practice

Making improvements, striving to do better, are wonderful things; but notice when you've pushed yourself too hard and have made attaining a goal a condition of your self-love. At that moment, whatever you are striving for has become counterproductive. Remember, you can't reach perfection, because you are already there.

Rekindling Harmony

While I love spending time with others, I also love being alone and enjoying the communion of my Personal Dream. That's good news! Because if I didn't enjoy being with myself, that would make for a difficult life, as I am the only person who is with me all the time.

In the moments you are alone and experience suffering, realize that only you can be causing it (there is no one else in the room!). Whatever reason the mind may give for your suffering, the underlying cause is disharmony of your Personal Dream.

How can you rekindle harmony? One way is to reengage yourself with the things that make you happy and make you enjoy being alive. Simply put, doing what you love is a path that leads straight out of suffering.

Remember, that is the point of all of this work: to enjoy life. It starts by enjoying the relationship you have with yourself.

Practice

Spend some time with yourself today, doing what you love to do. Notice how that colors the rest of your day with happiness.

A New Beginning

Imagine your most important relationships. Do you love these people because of who they really are, or do you love them because of who you *think* they are? The difference is enormous—it's oceans apart.

In the former, you actually have a relationship with someone close to you, one that is based on unconditional love and respect.

In the latter, you don't. You're dancing by yourself, imposing an image onto someone else, never seeing them for who they really are.

Heartbreak occurs the moment you see that the story you've told yourself about someone you say you love was just that—a story. With the truth revealed, all of a sudden the story comes crashing down.

But this truth, while painful, is also an opportunity for immense growth in the relationship, because now you are willing to see the person for who they really are.

Practice

Heartbreak does not have to be the end of a relationship. Rather, it can be a new and beautiful beginning based on unconditional love, respect, and truth. With awareness, remember that when you become willing to see yourself for who you really are, only then are you willing to see others for who they really are.

The Power of Your Mind

The human mind is a wonderful tool, a literal manufacturing plant of thought, and it has enabled us to create wonderful structures and develop amazing technologies over millennia.

But without awareness, our minds can take on more power than we might want by completely absorbing our attention. If we let it, the mind will constantly narrate, or commentate on, everything we do, say, see, touch, smell, taste, and hear. It is like taking a sip of wine and saying, "It's a bit dry; it has definitely aged well, but I can taste the bark. I've had better." Instead of simply experiencing the joy and flavors of the wine, we are analyzing the flavor, trying to break it down and fit it into a context and language we already know. In doing this, we miss out on much of the actual experience.

This is a simple example of how our mind can narrate life—by explanation, comparison, and judgment. Instead of taking an experience for what it is, we create a story to make it fit our beliefs.

Practice

Your mind is a wonderful tool, but balance is key in making sure you use the tool, instead of the tool using you. As you move through your day, be conscious and try to experience each moment anew, letting go of the impulse to narrate your experience on the spot and pass judgment.

Jealousy and Envy

When jealousy or envy hits, it is like a tidal wave that crashes through us and reveals the sticky mud of our insecurities, fears, and attachments. This always begins with the mental comparison that we are not being or having enough. If we are not careful, more subtle attacks of jealousy and envy can arise when we form agreements with society's messages that are continuously bombarding us throughout our day.

Turn on the TV, radio, or computer, and within a few moments you can notice that some message is telling you that in some way, shape, or form you are not enough.

Practice

Through awareness, realize that any time you feel jealous or envious of someone, at the core of this feeling is an agreement that "you are not enough." Nothing could be further from the truth. You are complete, total, perfect; the entire universe resides inside you.

Life Is a Movie, Part 1

Imagine you're in a darkened movie theater, and on the screen you're watching the story of your life. You're engaged by the drama, the suspense, the tender moments, until all of a sudden, you have a moment of realization: For the last several hours, you forgot you were watching a movie! You were so hooked, so invested, that you were no longer aware of reality; you thought the movie was you!

Practice

Remember that you are not the events or happenings that occur in your life. You are something far greater than that. Everything will come and go in front of you, but you remain the same. Remembering that life is like a movie is the equivalent of maintaining awareness.

Life Is a Movie, Part 2

Imagine that you're back in the movie theater, but this time you walk out of the movie you are in and into the one next door. A friend is watching her own movie and is totally oblivious to you. The movie looks familiar, but it's not yours. In fact, as you watch closely, you realize the movie has nothing to do with you. It's your friend's movie, and she's totally different in this movie from how she is in your own.

You jump, scream, and shout, doing everything you can to wake her up, but she's mesmerized; she doesn't hear you at all. Ultimately, you realize that you have no influence on her whatsoever! The movie is entirely hers.

Practice

You are constantly projecting your own version of reality, and you are solely responsible for your own Personal Dream. Any choice you make, any action you take, is yours alone. You fall into disillusionment any time you think otherwise.

Guilt

If guilt has any beneficial use, it can only be to let you know when you have gone against your own moral code. When you are aware, guilt is a tiny nudge that helps you find and stand in your integrity.

But for most of us, guilt resembles a sledgehammer that we use to punish ourselves. Any time we use guilt to punish ourselves for a past "crime" we deem unforgivable, we have, by definition, just separated ourselves from self-love and self-acceptance.

The good news is that nothing you have ever done is unforgivable. Such an act does not exist.

Practice

Looking back on the story of your life, what past actions are you holding against yourself? Go to the mirror and say aloud, "I forgive you. You were doing the best you could at the time." With awareness, you realize that guilt is a heavy burden that you no longer need to carry.

Creating Images

When we're in public, to fit in and be accepted, we often present an image of ourselves that we think others wish to see. This image reflects who we think we're supposed to be and how we think we're supposed to act. In reality, this image exists only in your mind. Trying to live up to that image only leads to suffering.

That's the problem with pursuing images—they're illusionary, and they can only take us away from the truth of who we really are.

As Jesus said in the Gospel of Thomas, "When you take off all your clothes and stomp on them, only then will you know Heaven on Earth." It wasn't our literal clothes that Jesus was talking about, but the images we have created for ourselves.

Practice

Notice when you present yourself to others in a way that is not how you really are. While you can still make a choice to do this, especially if it is for the benefit of the other person, the point is to be conscious of that choice. When it's not benefiting you or the other person, drop your image and be who you are.

Finding Our Own Fanaticism

Fanaticism describes a rigid attachment to knowledge with an excessive intolerance of opposing views. It is driven by a need to believe in something 100 percent. . . . Anything that contradicts or puts into question the sustainability of the belief is a direct threat, and a fanatic will defend the belief at any cost. Prejudice, intolerance, and violence are the instruments with which the belief is imposed onto the Dream of the Planet.

Regardless of how it can appear, the driving force behind fanaticism is not hate or anger, but rather an extreme form of conditional love for self and others. This is how any beautiful belief in the world can become lost in corruption, as knowledge controls a person's will for sake of its own existence.

—*THE FIVE LEVELS OF ATTACHMENT*

When our attachment to a belief increases, the question of *who we are* becomes directly linked to *what we know.* At the highest level of attachment, Fanaticism, every decision we make is controlled by our beliefs. We have lost the power of choice.

Practice

Today, look within yourself and see where and when you have been a fanatic. When you recognize Fanaticism in others, remember that they are not bad or evil; they are only confused due to their extreme attachment to an ideology.

Creativity as a Catalyst for Change

While every one of us is creating our Personal Dream all the time, many of us get stuck in the same daily routines. For example, we wake up every morning at the same time, brush our teeth the same way, have our usual cup of coffee, drive the same road to work, and so on.

When you recognize all the repetitive actions you take every day, many of them without awareness, it is easy to understand why making the larger changes of creating new thought patterns and beliefs, such as unconditional self-love and self-acceptance, can be so challenging. Just the simple act of making little changes in your daily routines can help you remember that you have a choice in how you live your life and remind you of the magnificent creator that you are.

Creativity comes naturally when we are living a life of awareness.

Practice

To walk down a new path of transformation, you must be willing to forge new trails. Ignore the call of the well-paved road and start looking for new possibilities and new visions. With awareness, call forth the genius of your playful creativity and do some things differently today.

Giving Permission

You can only be subjugated by another if you give them permission. If someone insults you, screams at you, or gossips about you, you can sit and listen to him without letting it affect you, because any effect others' opinions have requires your permission. And that permission comes the minute you believe another's words and agree with her judgments.

Consequently, subjugation to the will of another only occurs when you doubt yourself, forget your true internal power, and let imposing beliefs take control of your intent.

I am not oppressed today, because I do not give anyone permission to oppress me. I do not need anyone's approval to express myself today, as my unconditional self-love reflects the power of my intent, the source of my faith in myself.

I am worthy of my own freedom, and so are you.

Practice

With awareness, remember that no insult or judgment has any power over you unless you agree with it.

Honor Your Body

My father always told me, "Love is the perfect balance between gratitude and generosity."

One way to strengthen our love for ourselves is by honoring our body. Expressing gratitude for the body we have begins by accepting how our body looks at this very moment. Our body is the vehicle that allows us to perceive and create in the Dream of the Planet; our body serves us even when it is sick or hurt.

We will have this body throughout the span of our life, and it will change and evolve with time. It is perfect because it is alive, and it is the body we will use to express intent throughout the course of our life.

Practice

We cannot give what we do not have, and having a balance of gratitude and generosity for your body allows you to share your love with everyone else. Be generous to your body: nurture it, feed it, give it rest, and strengthen it. Your body is perfect just the way it is in this moment, despite any internal narration to the contrary.

Taking Stock of Your Beliefs

Our point of view, our perception, is what creates our reality. When we are attached to our beliefs, our reality becomes rigid, stagnant, and oppressive.

As with many things in life, this rigidity is much easier to see in others than in ourselves. But little, if anything, is gained from taking the inventory of another.

With awareness, we examine our own beliefs and ideas to see which have stagnated and are no longer serving us. Life will give us plenty of opportunities to do so.

Practice

The next time you hear yourself having a judgmental thought, either about yourself or another, ask yourself: "From what belief does this judgment originate? Is the belief still true for me, or is my judgment automatic?"

With awareness, remember that you have the power to change your mind; drop any belief that is no longer serving you.

You Always Have a Choice

Have you ever said, "I don't have a choice; I have to do it"? Statements like this are especially common when it comes to fulfilling the obligations we have adopted through the Dream of the Planet, such as work, school, or family life. But at the very core, this statement is an untruth, and it is the basis of all domestication. No matter what your circumstances may be, you always have a choice. Don't give it away by making the statement "I have to" and believing it.

Practice

Nothing breaks domestication like remembering you have a choice. Next time you feel obligated to do something, remember that you don't really have to unless you want to. If you choose to do the thing, say to yourself beforehand, "I want to do this."

There will no doubt be some situations in which you find yourself saying, "I don't want to." Guess what? You won't. Your choice will be exercised.

Being Free

If we are not careful, we can create a false image or projection of what it means to be "free" or what it means to be an individual who can love unconditionally.

When we attach ourselves to this image, we can corrupt the image by making it an ideal to live up to, rather than embracing where we find ourselves at each moment. For example, let's say a situation arises, and we are overtaken by jealousy. When an emotional reaction like this occurs that is different from our idealized image of unconditional love, we are tempted to believe in the false image of self and impose a condition that supports that image. We then judge ourselves for the emotional reaction, saying something like, "You should be more spiritual than that!" In this way, the noble image of freedom and unconditional love has become a tool of self-domestication.

But if we accept ourselves unconditionally, including the fact that we have just reacted, it allows us to free up our energy and move through the emotion, rather than stuffing it down by denying the truth. Unconditional acceptance gives us perspective, because we are no longer trying to blame or defend; we are simply accepting what is.

Practice

Welcome every aspect of yourself today. Forget the image of perfection that you may have created in your mind and realize that you are perfect in actuality.

Compassion versus Pity

In our society, the concepts of compassion and pity are often used interchangeably, without the realization that there are big differences between the two.

Compassion is having concern for the well-being of others while at the same time respecting their free will. It means being there for someone while respecting his or her strengths and capabilities. We maintain an open hand that is ready to help, but only if our friend asks for it.

Pity is feeling sorry for others and taking on and carrying their pain or trying to fix it for them. We're doing a tremendous disservice to someone if we never allow him or her to see the strength of his or her own intent. Pity is when we let our concern for others overtake us, and we want to step in, make decisions for them, and help them when they can and should be helping themselves. With pity, there is no respect.

Practice

With awareness, notice the difference between having compassion for others and taking pity upon others. The next time you find yourself projecting onto others how you think they should be, not honoring their right to make choices for themselves, make the choice to reserve judgment. Treat them with compassion instead.

Quieting the Judge

The word *Toltec* means "artist," and the canvas for a Toltec's art is life itself.

If you view life through the eyes of an artist, you will see that everything is a work in progress, a never-ending masterpiece. As the paint hits the canvas, it grows and develops, even if we don't always have an outline to keep us within the lines. Every brushstroke is perfect simply because it exists.

If you view life through the eyes of the judge and conditional love, then life is no longer a work of art; rather, it becomes a series of goals to achieve and contests to win. You are happy when things go "right" and upset when they go "wrong." Viewing life this way can make for a very difficult experience.

Practice

With awareness, notice how you view the ups and downs of life today. Are you trying to "win," or are you living in the realization that everything that occurs is an artistic creation of life? Be the artist, not the judge.

Playing Make-Believe

As children, many of us played make-believe games with our friends: cops and robbers, Barbies, superheroes, tea parties, and the like. In those games, we assumed the identity of a particular character, and for the duration of the game we pretended to be something we were not. But the second the game was over, we dropped that identity and went back to being our old selves.

As adults, we often play a version of make-believe in certain social situations. That is, we put on a mask and engage one another in a particular setting, perhaps at a cocktail party, a work function, or even a family event.

Sometimes the mask is needed to adapt to a group dynamic. A lot of times these masks are benign; we play the part of dutiful child, employee, or even "bestselling author," and when we are done we return to who we truly are. The problem occurs when we forget that we are wearing a mask, and we think the mask is who we truly are. Over time, these masks can become very heavy burdens and dropping them can be freeing.

Practice

What identities have you adopted for yourself? How do you portray those identities in the world? Who are you without the mask? Remember, there are situations where you may choose to put on a mask, and it's OK. Just don't forget it's just a mask!

Staying in Our Comfort Zone

It's not easy to let go of our identity—especially when the things we believe about ourselves (even those that cause us pain) provide a familiar comfort zone. But having a sense of personal importance that is contingent on knowledge, status, or any other temporary role we assume in life is vulnerable to collapse. Staying in our comfort zone may seem cozy for the moment, but the way to reality and awareness actually gets tougher the longer you maintain the status quo.

Eventually, through the continued practice of awareness, we find that who we are is far greater than any identity we have adopted. This realization that you are timeless and limitless is very powerful; it's like letting go of the railing when you are certain you are free from any danger of falling.

Practice

With awareness today, step outside your comfort zone, remembering that who you are is far greater than anything you know. Don't be afraid to try something new; remember that "failure" is impossible.

Keeping Projections at Bay

We create an image in our mind of how everyone, including ourselves, should behave. For example, if we catch a friend taking something personally, we might judge her for failing to live up to an ideal image of someone who "never takes things personally." Now we have two problems instead of one. Not only is our friend upset, but we're thinking they might be a little self-absorbed, too.

Instead, accept your friend's feelings and support her. It can be difficult not to project how you'd like to have things go over, but that's what unconditional love is all about.

Practice

Today, let go of the projected image you may have of someone close to you, and set yourself free of your own self-projected image in the process.

Allow yourself the opportunity to see others as they truly are, and let them love you for the person you are, the person you now love unconditionally.

Try repeating this affirmation today: "From this moment forth, I can give what I really have, and what I have is unconditional love that flows freely with every beat of my heart. I love you, and I say that with the complete freedom of life."

Labels

Your mind, like all minds, tends to identify and label things automatically: tree, stranger, yellow. Without realizing it, you then begin to anticipate what you are going to see next based on what you know. When this happens, your awareness grows duller, as the lazy brain overlooks distinctions. People lose their unique identity and richness, and experiences are compared to what "was" rather than being explored for what is now.

When you look at life without any labels or expectations, all the wonders of this precious moment reveal themselves.

Practice

To sharpen your awareness, notice the subtleties in things. Consciously look for differences rather than similarities. When you interact with someone you "know," act as if you are meeting them for the first time. Notice how they look, how they act; listen to what they say. This is a foundational practice of awareness.

Living in the Future

"What do you want to be when you grow up?" This is a fun and common question for adults to ask little children. But we can also identify this as one of the first examples of how we became domesticated to the idea that our life starts at some future point.

Too often we put off our own happiness until some event is realized the future. "I will be happy when I graduate from college/when I get married/when I get the right job/when I have children." The result is a cycle of setting and achieving milestones, only to realize after each one is achieved that it failed to do for us what we had thought it would. This is why many great masters of all traditions have stressed the importance of living in the present moment.

Practice

By practicing awareness you realize that happiness and joy exist in the present moment. If you can't find them here, you won't find them anywhere.

Engaging in Life

From the Toltec standpoint, a clean mirror is when you see every situation in life exactly as it is, unclouded by the smoke of your beliefs and viewpoints. From this place of clarity, you are aware that the act of engaging in life is an act of love; and consciously choosing the way you want to live is an act of unconditional love for yourself.

Approaching your life as a work of art based on self-love allows you to move in any direction you choose. You are not bound to others' domestication, nor do you feel the need to domesticate others to see things from your point of view. You consider your options, and your actions are genuine.

Practice

With awareness, you see every situation clearly, unclouded by the smoke of your beliefs. This allows you to take the best action for yourself out of self-love, and in so doing create a world of peace.

Seeing Fear for What It Is

Fear has just one function in life: to keep us safe from harm. When we are in real danger, fear protects us by telling us to freeze, fight, or flee. It is a normal emotion we've all experienced. But the fear that impedes us from living our life authentically is a different kind of fear. It is irrational fear, which occurs when we are not in real danger, but rather the danger only exists in the mind.

Practice

The next time you feel afraid, ask yourself if you are in any real danger. If you're not, you know that what you are afraid of is an illusion. Letting go of that illusion is an act of self-love, and it allows you to live in peace.

The Key to Transformation

Most of us don't live in a monastery or an ashram, surrounded by people who practice silence, meditation, or prayer constantly. Rather, we live in the Dream of the Planet, where we are continually interacting with people who are at various levels of awareness. As you interact with others and want to find harmony in those relationships, remember that the harmony starts with you.

As you become aware of yourself and love and accept yourself for who you are, you are then able to give to others what you hope to receive in return. Remember the old adages about leading by example, or that you cannot give what you do not have? It is only once you have unconditional love and acceptance for yourself that you will be able to give unconditional love and acceptance to others.

Practice

The key to all forms of transformation is awareness, and the starting point is accepting your truth and loving yourself exactly the way you are at this moment. With all the freedom of life, say to yourself, "I love you."

Misplaced Faith

Without realizing it, we put our faith in many external things. In fact, we have so much faith in some things that we take them for granted. For example, we have faith that when we go to sleep at night the sun will rise in the morning. When we flip the light switch, we have faith that a dark room will be illuminated. Many of us have faith in our closest friends and family members to be there in our times of need.

But the most important person you can have faith in is yourself. Unfortunately, this is what many people don't believe. Instead, they judge themselves, belittle themselves internally, and doubt their own abilities. When you look at it this way, it's no surprise that so many people are suffering in the world.

By believing in the power of you, you learn to trust your own decisions; and in so doing, you open up a world of new possibilities.

Practice

With awareness, remember that you have all your own answers. Sometimes you need others to help you find them, but the ultimate answer is inside you. With awareness, see that any direction in life is possible for you today.

Finding a New Melody

"I should, I should, I should."

"He shouldn't, she shouldn't, they shouldn't."

Think about your set of attached beliefs, your "shoulds" and your "shouldn'ts," as a unique melody repeating itself in your mind.

Are you constantly trying to force your melody onto other people's melodies? Do you do this without even realizing it? In some cases, the melody you're playing doesn't even originate with you, and sometimes it's not even the one you want to be hearing.

If you continue playing only what you know, you never open yourself to listen to the other songs flowing around you. In this way, you are letting your attachment to your particular melody, a.k.a. your beliefs, control you.

Practice

With awareness, listen to other people's melodies today. Perhaps you will learn something or contribute to them. At the very least, simply notice where the music takes you. By letting go of your attachment to what you think the melody *should* be, you open yourself to the potential to create a unique and beautiful composition of your own or a collaboration that can be shared with others.

Getting a Handle on Anger

Anger is a natural human emotion. No matter how spiritually evolved we may be, in a moment of great loss, betrayal, pain, or injustice, anger arises.

In many cases, our anger is accompanied by a "no" to whatever is happening at that moment. In this way, we are using anger to express our intent. Saying no from a place of anger can add force to our no; and for a moment we feel powerful. But this feeling of power is illusory, and it always leaves us with an emotional hangover of negativity after the anger subsides. It also causes suffering for those caught in its path.

The truth is that anger doesn't make us powerful at all; in fact, by communicating our intent through anger, we are actually giving our power away.

With awareness, we realize we don't need the crutch of anger to effectively express our intent. We can say no from a place of calmness, even in the subtlest way, because we know that the mere mention of it has expressed the power of our own intent.

Practice

Imagine someone yelling emphatically, gesturing wildly, and bullying to get their point across, versus someone who's calm, collected, and communicating clearly and with intention. Who do you think has the *real* power in that situation?

The next time you notice yourself getting angry, try to wait until the anger subsides prior to manifesting your intent.

Taking Time to Heal

Our emotional wounds, large and small, feed the "parasite" of the mind, as our attention is consumed by the negative thoughts that feed off that wound.

When this relationship between the mind and the emotional body is focused on past hurt, the parasite thrives as it uses the emotional wound to keep us trapped in a fog of negativity.

Forgiveness heals any wound, and as the wound heals, the parasite can no longer use it to cause us pain. To forgive is to accept and let go. We can learn from the experience that caused the wound, and even cry if the wound is still painful in our emotional body, but forgiveness stops the parasite from feeding on the wound and using it to reinforce a condition in our mind.

Practice

Every wound heals in time, and giving yourself time to heal is an expression of compassion for yourself, an act of love.

Be gentle with yourself today.

Being Aware of the Messages

Television, radio, the Internet, as well as books and magazines can be wonderful tools to help you learn, and they provide entertainment in the Dream of the Planet. But if you aren't careful, they can also pull you out of awareness and draw you into the pit of suffering.

Remember that every time you engage in media, you are allowing your mind to be hooked into someone else's dream. By paying attention to these external messages, you can discover which dreams are inspiring you, and which are feeding your stories of self-judgment, conditional love, and domestication.

Everyone is sharing their art in words, symbols, images, and stories. It's your choice which art you allow into your creation and make a part of your Personal Dream.

Practice

With awareness, notice how you feel when a television show, website, or book really hooks your attention. Which stories draw you into suffering? Which raise your vibration and support your highest good?

Seeing the Power of Your Intent

You are always manifesting something. Notice how with every action, from taking a breath to moving your arms, through every thought, verbal or nonverbal, you are making something *happen*. You are initiating change.

The mind will often label simple actions as unremarkable. But the reality is that we are all miracle makers, and we manifest miracles in every moment through the power of intent.

Practice

Today, become aware of how you express your intent and how you are able to manifest the whole world with the simplest of actions. You are alive!

Letting Go
of the Need to Be Right

There comes a point in life when we grow tired of needing to be right—especially when we see how this ego-feeding need affects our most meaningful relationships. Our attachments don't let us see further than the tips of our own noses; they obscure our relationships with the beautiful souls who just want to be our friends or love us.

The good news is, as we become aware of how our filter of knowledge is constructed, we realize that lasting change only comes from within. This is a big responsibility, but it means releasing these attachments and filters is absolutely possible for each and every one of us.

Practice

Next time you find yourself taking a stand and valuing your ego over truth or collaboration, take a step back and ask yourself: "Would I rather be right or happy?" Oftentimes our disagreements can be resolved without us needing to be right 100 percent of the time.

Staying Strong
in Times of Adversity

Over the course of our lives, situations will arise that can sometimes seem insurmountable. When I'm faced with obstacles and life seems really difficult, my unconditional love for myself gives me the strength to continue.

I greet the ups and downs of life's journey with unconditional love for myself and the people in my life by understanding that I am only truly alive in the present moment; the future is a projection that does not yet exist.

As long as there is life, everything is possible.

Practice

With awareness, remember to love yourself and others unconditionally when the road gets tough. Only through love can you overcome obstacles with peace.

The Authentic Self

As you engage life, your awareness is like a flower, continuously opening and closing as you move through your day. Awareness and attachment have an inverse relationship; that is, as you lose your awareness, you increase your attachment. As you become more aware, your attachments become fewer and weaker.

Regardless of how attached you become to any belief or idea, *you are always your Authentic Self;* you just simply forget that when you step away from awareness.

Practice

Many religious and spiritual traditions in the world have created disciplines that allow you to remain in a state of harmony and stay aware of your Authentic Self: prayer, meditation, yoga, chanting, dancing, and many others. If you engage in any of these wonderful practices, remember that the goal of all of them is to anchor you in awareness.

The Actions of Others

One of the biggest drains on your energy is making other people's actions about you. Other people's actions are always about them; they do things based on their point of view and their Personal Dream.

So when you take something someone does or says and make it about you—that is, take something personally—you are forming an agreement that what they are saying is also true for you.

Practice

The mechanism of defense is a signal that you are taking something personally, and you have formed an agreement with someone else's words or actions. When you notice yourself having a defensive reaction, that is an indicator that you believe what they are saying or doing might be right. If they are right, the quickest way to peace is to own it, and make any changes in yourself that you feel necessary. If they are not right, let their words slide off like rain off an umbrella.

Equality

The main job of the ego is to protect the false image of a separate self. One way it accomplishes this is by reinforcing the illusion of personal importance.

Internal voices that say, "I am better than you" or "I have more than you" represent a deep undercurrent of personal importance in our society. Our collective egos have set up many mechanisms to support these inaccurate notions, and pursuing these false ideals leads to unhealthy comparisons, competition, and ultimately violence in our human family.

Awareness is the key to exposing this illusion, and unconditional love is the antidote. You, I, and everyone else in the world are equal. We are all expressions of consciousness. We are One. When we love one another without conditions, we create a dream of perfect harmony. I call it heaven on earth.

Practice

With awareness today, remember that everyone you see, everyone you meet, everyone you interact with is a part of you. What you do to another you also do to yourself. Loving and recognizing the equal divinity in all beings is recognizing the divinity in yourself.

Seeing You Have Options

Life always gives us a choice, even when we don't realize it. Whatever is happening in our lives, our choice lies in how we respond. Without awareness, we fall into our automatic reactions or habits, and we surrender that choice. This is the difference between "I have to" and "I want to."

For example, I've chosen to go to work because I have chosen to fulfill that responsibility in my life. If I see working through the filter of "I have to," then it will be difficult for me to enjoy what I am doing, because I am relinquishing choice and forcing myself to do something. But if I see working through the filter of "I want to," it is because I have placed my intent in that direction; I am working willingly. Remembering this makes all the difference in the world. Recognize you always have a choice, and once you've made a decision, follow through without resistance. You don't "have to" do anything; but you do choose to do many things, for many different reasons.

Practice

What do you choose to do today? No matter what happens, good or bad, be aware that you have a choice about how you'll respond. With awareness, see your daily activities as opportunities to choose how you want to proceed in life.

The Parasite and the Ally

We all have voices in our minds—words, thoughts and stories that have the power to fill us with inner sunshine or smother us with mental smog. When you listen to the voices in your head, do you hear words of fear and judgment and stories that cause inner conflict and struggle? Or do you hear words of support, unconditional love, and self-acceptance? The former voice is like a parasite attempting to drain you of your energy. The latter is your ally, as it sees the beautiful being that you are.

Transform your inner voice to be your best friend by shifting every internal conversation toward the positive, one word at a time.

Practice

With awareness, notice the different voices that speak to you throughout the day. One speaks truth, the other lies. You can tell the difference by noticing how you feel when the voice speaks. Your ally will never lead you astray.

Assuming

If you see three quarters of a circle, even though a quarter is missing, you can still recognize the shape as a circle. The same is true if you see two sides of a triangle. Based on past experiences, the mind supplements incomplete new information with the beliefs it is already attached to and assumes it knows the future.

While making assumptions about geometric shapes doesn't have serious consequences, when it comes to human interactions, assumptions based on past experiences can wreak havoc on our lives. The everyday word for this kind of assumption is prejudice. While it is often associated with race or sex or creed, the prejudices of the mind go far beyond that.

For example, if we meet someone with a very expensive car or house, do we make assumptions about their character? If we meet someone in a professional setting, or a soup kitchen, what assumptions might we make about them?

Practice

With awareness, notice the assumptions and prejudices the mind makes today. Becoming aware of our automatic prejudices is the first step in releasing them.

Shedding Artifice

Your name and the body it represents in the Dream of the Planet are empty symbols whose meaning and definition are the expression of your intent as you live life. The *true you* is the living being, the point of perception, that gives these symbols life.

Oftentimes we confuse our bodies and our names with who we really are, and the result is suffering.

You are not your body, and you are not the label attached to it. You are life; you are love. You are the source of love, and, consequently, you have enough love to share with everyone along the path of your life.

Your name and body represent the expression of love your intent has manifested.

Practice

Be the love that you are today. Consider that your name, your identity, and your appearance are just expressions of who you are, through your manifested love. Shed your body and your name and imagine what the true you might look like.

Being the Bully

When you understand domestication and the role it plays in relationships, you come to understand that an argument is simply an attempt to domesticate another to your own point of view.

Bullying is simply imposing on someone else how you think they should act, think, or be—you're asserting that your belief system is superior. You assume the role of a movie director in the life of another, telling him or her, "This is the part I want you to play, and this is how I want you to behave." While we can decide which part we'd like to play in our own life, we can't make that decision for someone else.

An argument is a byproduct of conditional love.

Practice

When we see an argument for what it is (an attempt to domesticate another to our point of view), it becomes much easier to not have one. The next time you find yourself in an argument, ask yourself: How am I trying to domesticate this person? How will his or her domestication strengthen my ego and sense of personal importance? What belief am I trying to protect?

When we love others unconditionally, we can still disagree, but it is very unlikely our disagreements will become arguments.

Realizing Your
Infinite Potential

There are 360 degrees of possibilities surrounding you. This point—this now—is your potential. To move forward in any direction is to make a choice; you say yes to something and no to all else. This is true regardless of whether or not you are aware of the infinite possibilities present in each moment.

The more attached you are to something, the more your vision is obscured and narrowed, sometimes to the point at which you are convinced that there is only one way to proceed. Your attachment to a belief cuts off your ability to see beyond that one possibility. So, as you consciously choose to let go of attachments that no longer work for you, your options seem to grow and expand. But what you are really doing is increasing your perspective, as all possibilities were there all along.

Practice

Today, remember that all possibilities are available to you in life; the only confinements are the chains you have put on yourself. Choose now to discard those chains.

Forgiveness

In the current Dream of the Planet, domestication is a reality for almost everyone. In most cases, it is also necessary. Without some form of domestication, we would be unable to function in society. This is why my father sometimes tells new parents: "Be sure to domesticate your kids before someone else does."

Even if you don't have kids, you were a kid once, and you were domesticated accordingly. Remember this as you think about those who domesticated you. They were trying to help you survive in our world, and it worked. Seeing it this way makes it easier to forgive. They were doing the best they could at the time.

Practice

With awareness, try to forgive anyone who ever attempted to domesticate you to his or her own point of view. Their efforts were nothing personal; they were just doing their best at the time. You can now choose for yourself what behaviors and beliefs are true for you. This is the definition of being a grown-up.

Changing with Love

When we let go of our judgments and criticisms and accept ourselves as we are, conditional love will no longer be the motivator that compels us to change, but rather love being expressed in the form of passion will be. When we love what we do, we let inspiration flow through us to envision what can be, and we make the choice to manifest it with our talents. Passion will be the motivator that allows us to follow through with what we are able to envision. It is an act of love.

Practice

Accept and love yourself completely as you are today. From this point, any change you make is from a place of self-love, not fear or self-condemnation. As a result, the change is much more likely to transform into passion, and any outcome is perfect because the journey was enjoyable.

Playing It Safe

When we stay in our safety zones where we feel comfortable and secure, we become firmly entrenched in a this-is-who-I-am mindset. From this perspective, the worst thing imaginable is change. The structures we've put so much time and effort into maintaining would all go away, and that would be terrible.

Yet this happens again and again in varying degrees throughout our lives. When I believe something must stay in its rightful place, exactly as it is, for me to be OK, I have become attached to it; I have confused this external thing with who I am.

If that external thing changes, and eventually everything does, how do you react? If you have placed your sense of self in it, then you have to defend it. You have to argue for it. You have to come up with definitions and meaning. In short, you have created an attachment.

Practice

With awareness, notice that nothing outside you defines who you are. The life force that is you cannot be fulfilled by external objects; only the ego tries to make the finite infinite, and the result is suffering.

With this knowledge, try something new today.

Letting Each Relationship
Stand on Its Own

Every relationship is unique, as are the individuals who are in it; it has never existed before, and the remnants of any prior relationship are only in your memory.

Without awareness, you can allow the remnants of a past relationship to affect a current one. You can hold on to a point in the past and project it onto your present relationship, thus affecting the new relationship with something that has nothing to do with it. Or you can learn from that same point and let past experiences contribute to your maturing mind as you engage your present relationship with unconditional love, letting it evolve with its own moments.

Being aware of the difference between projecting and learning not only allows us to enjoy the relationship we are in, it also allows us to communicate with one another with clarity as we build the Dream of Us.

Practice

Remember to see every relationship you are in as unique. While it is beneficial to learn from past relationships, you don't want to project prior experiences. Doing so keeps you stuck in the past and closes you off to the beauty of what's happening right now.

Engaging in the Dream of the Planet

Together we engage in the Dream of the Planet, as we give solidity and shape to form through our mutual intent. Whether this dream is the perfect nightmare or the most harmonious utopia depends upon the relationship between our minds and what we create through our agreements.

Remember that whatever love you are withholding from others in the Dream of the Planet you are also withholding from yourself. Loving yourself unconditionally allows you to love others unconditionally, and vice versa. Only when you have unconditional love for yourself can you bring this love to the Dream of the Planet.

Peace starts with you.

Practice

With awareness, make peace the focus of your day. Engage with others with a sense of oneness, remembering that the love you send out into the world becomes a part of the Dream of the Planet. Support others as they offer unconditional love to you as well.

Domestication and the Ego

Domestication and the ego work hand in hand. Domestication rewards the ego with conditional love when perfection is achieved through the eyes of the judge, and it punishes the ego with self-rejection when we fall short of our own expectations.

It's a vicious cycle.

After years of repetition, the ego is artificially strengthened through domestication, and it works diligently to protect the rules of our domestication by constantly reminding us that our worthiness is tied to achieving this false image of perfection.

The key to breaking the cycle is unconditional self-love. When we love ourselves no matter what, we expose the ego and the system of domestication for what it is: a falsehood.

Practice

With awareness today, notice the moment you hear the voice of punishment inside yourself. When this occurs, stop immediately and instead say to yourself: "This is who I am, and I love myself without conditions."

The Art of Not
Taking Things Personally

We do not need to defend ourselves or our beliefs against other people's opinions and beliefs. Our only need is self-respect. When we have self-respect, we do not take what other people say and do personally.

If we give in to the temptation to make someone else's actions a personal affront, we have lost that self-respect by saying yes to their agreement. Once we do this, the attachment to this belief makes it necessary for us to switch our motive from one of defense to offense. With one shift, we can easily go from being victim to aggressor, which has a whole new set of consequences.

By not taking things personally, we do not give in to our sense of personal importance and can therefore make decisions based on mutual respect, which will solve problems instead of making them worse.

Practice

Like the Toltec hunter, be aware of your reactions today. Through the practice of awareness, any perceived attack on you will fall off like a loose garment.

Coming into Your Own

Most of us have mentors in our lives who nurture us as we grow, igniting our passions and illuminating our capabilities as they share their wisdom in the form of knowledge.

There comes a point when we must step out of our mentor's shadow, when we are ready to go out on our own. Courage and trust in ourselves give us the strength to take this important step, the step that lets us know we are capable of anything our intent is able to express.

But we always remember there is still more to learn. Everyone we come into contact with can teach us something. Everyone we meet is a personification of all the great masters—Jesus, Buddha, Moses, Krishna, Muhammad, and so on.

Practice

Follow your own compass today, being in the world with a willingness to learn. Remember that every person you meet is a representation of the Divine, a manifestation of the Authentic Self, and can teach you something. Some teach us what to do; others teach us what not to do.

Discerning the Messages

The Fifth Agreement is "Be Skeptical, but Learn to Listen." Be skeptical because most of what you hear isn't true. You know that humans speak with symbols, and that symbols aren't the truth. Symbols are only the truth because we agree, not because they are really truth.

—DON MIGUEL RUIZ & DON JOSE RUIZ, THE FIFTH AGREEMENT

Society sends such loud messages about how we should dress, act, be, and so on that we can get lost in the multitude of messages, forgetting we have a choice with which, if any, we will agree.

When our attention gets hooked into the world, we often make the mistake of agreeing with the status quo without even realizing we have done so. This is one way in which practicing the Fifth Agreement—"Be skeptical, but learn to listen"—can be very helpful.

Simply put, the Fifth Agreement can be translated as "I'm willing to listen to the messages, but I reserve the ability to scrutinize what I'm hearing; that is my privilege. I will decide if any message I hear is ultimately true for me."

The ability to have scrutiny—that is, to be skeptical—is the ability to separate yourself from any message that you hear. You are then able to receive the message in an objective manner and consciously choose if you wish to agree with it or not.

Practice

With awareness today, notice the many messages and ideas that you are bombarded with on a routine basis. As these come in, ask yourself, "Is that true for me?" and see what answer comes. You may be surprised by some of the answers!

Kindness

A wise man once said, "The three most important things to do in life are: be kind, be kind, be kind."

Kindness comes from generously opening your heart and seeing everyone as a friend deserving of consideration. Cultivating kindness is a powerful spiritual practice that grows as you nourish kindness inside yourself. When you get rushed or feel upset, it's even more important to practice kindness. Kindness will slow you down, create connection, and bring a smile to your face and to the faces of those you connect with.

Practice

With awareness, practice treating yourself and others with kindness today. Remember that everyone is always doing his or her best, and let your words and actions be considerate of their journey, as well as your own.

Finding Your One True Love

According to the Dream of the Planet, to be "in love" we must have someone to love. And, of course, that person is supposed to love us back. We get really hung up on this last part! This kind of love has so many conditions attached to it that suffering is inevitable. Not only that, but we also forget the biggest love of our life in the process: ourselves! When we look in the mirror and cannot see a reflection of love, it means smoke has distorted our view and made us think that love is something that needs to be gained or earned.

Practice

There is no need for you to chase love when you are love. Anytime you are not feeling love for yourself, the key is to release your attachment to whatever negative belief is keeping you from experiencing the love that you are. Find that belief and release it. When you look deeply into yourself, the true image of love will appear.

The Real versus the Imagined

Instead of simply experiencing love, being love, our narrators explain how love should feel: what makes us worthy of love; who should love us and how they should express it; what we need to do or achieve to love ourselves; and what others need to do to receive our love in return.

When we begin to believe the narrators' analysis of what love should be and become attached to that belief, we begin to impose it on ourselves and others, thus creating a distorted reflection of love. The narrators can convince us that if we can achieve an imagined perfection, we will be so full of love that life will be smooth going from that point on. But what has really happened is we have just made love conditional.

Practice

Unconditional love occurs the moment we stop labeling, judging, and discerning that which appears in our field of awareness. Everything is perfect exactly as it is. This includes you, too.

Let Go and Let God

Sometimes we can't fix what has been broken. The act of surrender is accepting that truth. This can be very difficult to do when our grief is so strong that it won't let us see any other possibility.

Be gentle with yourself in these moments. Nothing is gained by denying your feelings, forcing them into your subconscious. Remember that you have to feel your emotions and honor them for them to pass.

If we look deeply into any situation that appears to be broken, we can see that nothing is ever really lost. It may take time, but as our emotions subside, we can begin to see the different possibilities still present before us.

Practice

With awareness today, practice the art of surrender: let go. Life begins again with every breath, and happiness sprouts in your heart with each step forward, as you become aware once again of your full potential.

The Origin of Your Action

Action is our ability to create the world we want and to engage others in the Dream of the Planet. It is the manifestation of our intent.

In our interactions with others, it is inevitable that sometimes we'll disagree about the best way to proceed in anything. This is unavoidable in human relationships, and it's OK. When you take action or engage others with whom you have a disagreement, the most important thing to keep in mind is your intent.

Before taking any steps in defending your position, ask yourself: Am I coming from a place of love or a place of fear? Only when our intent comes from a place of love rather than a place of fear do we create peace in the world and in ourselves.

Practice

With awareness today, notice the intent of your actions. Do you speak and act from a place of love or from a place of fear? You're more likely to be understood in an argument, and will find reconciliation more quickly, if you can communicate from a place of love.

Finding Your Own Fanaticism

When we are aware of the divine spark that exists inside us, we can go to any church, any synagogue, any temple, any mosque, any drum circle, and always find the grace of God.

But oftentimes we see those who have become so attached to a set of religious beliefs that they adopt the mindset, "My religion is right, and yours is wrong." Most of us can easily see this level of fanaticism in others, but it's far more challenging to spot this in ourselves. For instance, beliefs about eating only organic food, using homeopathic medicine, lifestyle choices, and the like are all areas in which, if we are not careful, our attachment to the "rightness" of them can become fanatical; when we allow this, we corrupt the original noble inspiration.

Practice

With awareness, notice the viewpoints that you are so attached to you think everyone should feel the same way. When others don't agree with you, this is an opportunity to show your love and respect by letting them think and act for themselves. The good news is that you will release your own attachments in the process, and let their beautiful traditions become alive as you let go of the distorted filter of fanaticism.

The Energy of Life

Computers are incredible things. They are a combination of hardware, which can be touched, designed, and quantified, and software, which has no physical mass but can be changed to make the hardware execute certain functions, such as printing, displaying images, and recording keystrokes.

However, one additional thing is necessary to bring the computer to life: electricity. This invisible power is what makes the computer different from a rock, because without electricity, a computer is just another object. The electricity brings a computer to life, allowing it to function and perform. Shut off the flow of electricity, and the computer becomes lifeless.

Your physical body is like the hardware of a computer, and your brain is like the software. You can change the hardware (body) or the software (mind) to run more efficiently and do some incredible things, but without awareness, this body and mind are no different from a rock.

Practice

With awareness today, remember that you are not your body—you aren't even your mind. You are much, much more. You are the life force, the awareness, that gives life to your body and your mind.

The Power of Intent

The moment we realize the power of our intent is the moment we become free.

The person you were in the past, even just a day ago, no longer exists. The person you will be in the future does not yet exist. The real you can only be found in this very moment.

Who you will become in the future will be the result of your actions now. This is the power of your intent. When you say yes to something, it will be created. When you say no to something, it will not be created. Knowing this, make choices with awareness and say yes only to the things you truly want to manifest.

Practice

Today, remember the real power in choice: everything is possible. With awareness, say to yourself, "The decisions I make today will create my experience in the future."

Respecting Others' Point of View

No one else in the world thinks or feels exactly the same way you do about life. To think and to feel is an individual experience. As a result, no two people will have the same point of view.

Sometimes our viewpoints are so closely aligned that the differences aren't readily apparent. Other times, our viewpoints are so far apart it may seem difficult to find any common ground. The key to respecting the opinions of others is to have an open mind toward your own point of view.

When you look at your beliefs and viewpoints with openness, it becomes clear how attached you are to them. Without an open mind, you will constantly try to subjugate others to your own point of view, oftentimes without even realizing it. Being aware of your level of attachment to your own beliefs, ideas, and point of view allows you to respect the thoughts and feelings of others.

Practice

With awareness, examine your own beliefs and viewpoints the next time you disagree with someone. Although you may not change your viewpoint, being open to other possibilities and perspectives will allow you to respect the viewpoint of the other person.

Unconditional Self-Acceptance

Any time you look at yourself in the mirror and see a physical characteristic that you don't like, it is because you have made an agreement, such as "that's not pretty" or "that's not acceptable." According to your agreement, this characteristic is preventing you from looking the way you think you're "supposed" to look.

An extreme example of this is someone who is anorexic or bulimic; an agreement has been made that says being thin and being beautiful are equivalents. Even if this person is already fifteen pounds underweight, the agreement is so strong that it greatly distorts what he or she sees in the mirror.

This example is helpful because we can clearly see the detrimental nature of the agreement. But for many of us, our negative self-judgment regarding our physical appearance is harder to spot; sometimes because we're so used to it that we take it for granted—we have accepted our own self-judgments as fact!

Practice

Look at yourself in the mirror. If you hear the voices of self-judgment about some characteristic of your physical appearance, know that the way to peace and happiness is not through changing any physical feature, but rather through changing your agreements. You are perfect exactly the way you are at this moment. Every single characteristic of you is divine.

Look into the mirror and say the words, "I love you. You are beautiful exactly the way you are."

What's in a Name?

A symbol represents an idea or concept whose definition and meaning are subjugated to an agreement between individuals or communities. Symbols are great shortcuts and help in communicating with one another, but we should keep in mind the tendency to give symbols inherent power that they don't really have.

For example, your name is a symbol that allows you to be identified as an individual expression of consciousness in the Dream of the Planet. But as with any symbol, a name is only a pointer to the truth; it is not the truth itself.

When I introduce myself, I say, "I am Miguel." That is convenient and customary in our mutual dream. But I know that it is not completely who I am, for the essence of who I am is far, far greater than any name can describe. The same is true for you.

Practice

With awareness today, remember that your name and identity are helpful symbols, but they do not define you. Who you are is an individual manifestation of the one life, not subject to any symbol.

Following Your Passion

What do you love? The answer to this question is as diverse as the seven billion individuals in the world, and every single answer is correct for each individual.

When we pursue the activities we love, we fill our lives with joy and create a ripple of positive energy for those with whom we come into contact. But too often the old familiar voice of self-judgment pipes up, saying things like, "that will never work" or "you aren't being realistic" or, finally, "if you do that, you will fail."

Through awareness, you will notice that this voice did not—could not—have originated with you. These seeds of self-doubt were planted in your mind a long time ago. The purpose of this investigation is not to find and blame the farmers, but rather to see that your true nature will always encourage you to follow your heart.

Practice

Take time today to follow your passion. You will know that something is true for you when you do it, because you will feel alive.

Seeing More
than Body and Mind

Just as I am not this body, I am also not this mind. Our minds are malleable because our ideas, our sense of self, change based on our experiences. Our mind adapts because it's meant to adapt. We don't lose ourselves when we change our minds!

So while the mind changes, there is still a part of us that does not change. I'm still me, and you're still you.

Of course, one aspect of this work and the work of other great spiritual traditions is to clean up your mind. It's like doing maintenance on your car: You change the oil, and the car runs better. It's the same with your mind. When you filter out the negativity, the judgments, the conditional love, it feels so much better to have a clear mind.

But no matter how clean and refined your mind gets, you eventually come to realize that the mind is only a part of you, not who you actually are.

Practice

Notice the aware presence that exists behind your thoughts, behind your mind. The real you is this aware presence, the space in which your mind operates.

Being the Artist

My father often says, "Our life is a canvas, and we are all Picassos."

But what does this mean?

Viewing life through the eyes of an artist means accepting that everything you do is a work in progress, a never-ending masterpiece. Every brushstroke is perfect simply because it exists. As the paint hits the canvas, the picture grows and develops into what it is—even if we don't always have an outline to keep us within the lines. Whether colorful scribbles or a detailed landscape, each element of the piece is fulfilling and complete, even as we continue to paint, changing and evolving with every stroke of life.

Practice

As you move through life today, see everything that occurs as perfect and understand that making a mistake is simply not possible. Approaching life this way allows you to practice unconditional self-love. You love the artist, and you love the art you create.

The Party

Imagine you're at a party with a thousand people, and everyone is drunk except for you. As you look around, you see that everyone is acting crazy and disoriented; they are not seeing clearly. What's more, they all think you are drunk, too!

How would you deal with people in this situation? It would be pointless to try to reason with them or to try to convince them of anything. It would be equally pointless to take any of their actions seriously, as they are clearly out of their minds. You may choose to pretend to be drunk just to fit in.

Many others in the Dream of the Planet are so trapped in the fog of the mitote (the thousand voices that occupy the mind, all of which are vying for our attention) that they don't know who they really are. They act out in various ways, a prisoner of their own ego.

Practice

With awareness, realize that while others may think and act irrationally, you can maintain clarity. At times when you feel like you are being tested by the group, don't forget who you really are.

True Motivation

As we become familiar with how we have been domesticated by others, as well as how we have domesticated ourselves, we can look at the motivation behind every action we take and form new agreements that reflect how we actually wish to live our lives.

For instance, when you love what you do, it doesn't matter what the end results are, because you love the process. In this case, any outcome is a successful one, because you love the very action behind it. But if you're doing something only for the end result, and you dislike the process, that's a good indication that you are acting based on domestication and not sincere interest.

Practice

With awareness, notice why you do the things you do. You will find that you do some of the things in part because of your domestication. Once you've identified these things, remember to be gentle with yourself; change does not occur overnight.

Stepping Outside Your Story

Many spiritual traditions instruct you to be the observer, the witness, to your mind. But what exactly does this mean? You become an observer once you are able to step outside your own story, your inner thoughts and beliefs, and see things from a different perspective.

Being able to watch your own thoughts and beliefs provides an opportunity to question and reassess any idea or belief you have. Remember, you have a choice at every juncture to either continue to believe or not, and it's helpful to check in and reassess if what you say you believe is up to date.

Ultimately, being the observer shows us that we are not our thoughts or beliefs, but rather the aware presence in which thoughts and beliefs occur. In this role, we become aware of the thoughts we tell ourselves and decide anew if we still agree with them. This is especially helpful when we no longer want to believe the judgments of our conditional love.

Practice

Today, remember that thoughts come and go. You do not have to agree with every one of them. With awareness, you can form new agreements in your mind that serve your higher purpose, as well as consciously renew old agreements that still ring true.

Redefining Perfection

In the Toltec tradition, seeing life through the "eyes of the judge" is synonymous with defining perfection as something that is free from flaws. When we view life in this way, everything and everyone we see is subject to our judgments of how things could be perfect—including ourselves.

This is how we impose conditional love on ourselves, and others, as judgments are formed to punish and domesticate, imposing a condition for the worthiness of our acceptance and love.

But a flaw only means what we think it is; its meaning and interpretation are subject to an agreement. This is why there is such a deep truth in the statement, "We are perfectly imperfect."

Practice

With awareness, notice when you see life today through the "eyes of the judge." You, I, and everyone else are perfect exactly the way we are at this moment.

Awareness is the first step to change.

Active Listening

Many people want to share their opinions about how they think we should live our lives. Sometimes it feels as if we are being pulled in multiple directions based on these opinions, and our main task is to stay in our center.

Remember that opinions are not facts, and we can choose which, if any, we agree with. When someone close to you gives you advice, the important thing is to listen and honor the person by respecting his or her point of view. Respecting someone else's opinion does not mean you will agree with it.

With awareness, we listen and evaluate the opinions of others, but ultimately the choice of how we live rests squarely on our own shoulders. We know that our inner voice will guide us along the path we have chosen.

Practice

With awareness today, listen to the voice within. While others can teach you a lot as they offer their unique perspectives, remember to be true to yourself. Listen to others with care, but listen to your own voice with care as well.

Fear as a Paralyzer

Sometimes, it's not the obvious fears that hinder your joy, but the ones that are below the surface, just out of view. If you find yourself sabotaging your happiness, procrastinating on your dreams, or dismissing your achievements, it's likely that a hidden fear is at play.

When you take the flashlight of your awareness and shine it on the shadowy places where fear resides, you can see that the fears are so often like puffs of smoke. They appear solid at first, but when they are brought into the light, they dissipate into nothingness. Be courageous and stop to face your fears. Stop feeding your doubt and insecurity and instead dedicate yourself to nourishing your inspiration and passion.

Practice

When you find yourself feeling anything less than joyful, ask yourself, "What am I afraid of that is keeping me from experiencing the perfection of this moment?" Once the fear is identified, you will find it is about some future event, as all fear is. With awareness, remember that you are perfect exactly as you are; you have nothing to be afraid of, because the real you cannot be harmed.

Loving in the Moment

Loving everyone unconditionally, including ourselves, is the key to peace.

Yet we often find it easier to practice unconditional love with strangers than with members of our own family—and that includes ourselves. Why is that? One reason is that with those closest to us, we carry the baggage of "wrongs" from the past and project them into the now. With strangers, there is no baggage from the past, no emotional hooks to distract us from experiencing the perfect love that exists in the moment. This is why forgiveness and letting go of the past are so important. When we are ready to do so, it allows the opportunity to heal the wounds that divide us. Loving ourselves unconditionally also allows us to accept the truth that we may not be ready to forgive and let go. Respect starts with ourselves.

Practice

With awareness, remember to see everyone in your life as new in this moment. The person sitting at the dinner table with you today is not the same person who sat there yesterday. You are not the same person you were yesterday, either. Forgiveness allows us to love everyone for who they are at this moment.

Changing the World

My father has a saying that he uses fairly frequently: "Help me to change the world." It's a beautiful endeavor meant to focus our attention, love, and compassion on ourselves and everyone else in the world. But you can't change the world by pretending to be something you are not. Through this pretense, you are already rejecting yourself.

The very first step is to accept yourself just the way you are, "flaws" and all. Here is the irony: The moment you accept yourself is the moment you realize that whatever you thought was flawed is not flawed, and you change only because you want to, not because you have to.

Practice

With awareness, remember that the moment you accept yourself just the way you are is the moment you begin to change the world. You cannot give what you do not have. You cannot give love and respect to your brothers and sisters without first learning to love and respect yourself, just the way you are. There is no such thing as a flaw in any individual, and that includes you. Everyone is simply expressing his or her own intention in life.

Being in Awe

As adults, we can easily forget how amazing the world is. We get caught up in work, worry, self-doubts, and fears. Our days can become heavy with responsibility, and we forget to look up and see the beauty of the world around us.

Young children are great models of one key ingredient that fosters lightness and joyful awareness: awe. When you tap into that childlike wonder of how things work and look, when you are in awe of the totality of creation, you dissolve negativity and stress and replace them with delightful presence.

Practice

With awareness, look at the world around you with new eyes. Find amazement for the little things: the perfect red of a strawberry, the door handle that opens your car, the stapler at work. Let the magnificence that is life fill you up today.

Removing the Masks

I engage in the Toltec tradition by choice, fully aware that the name Toltec refers to an action or agreement belonging to a philosophy. I choose to call myself a Toltec, but I am aware that not calling myself a Toltec wouldn't lessen my agreement or the lessons I have learned from this tradition.

This is true for any identity you choose to adopt. Remember that you are the power that gives life to the identity, the mask you choose to wear. Suffering arises when we forget this and make the mask more important than our Authentic Self. In this way, we give our power to whatever identity we have chosen to adopt, no matter how noble we may think it is.

With awareness, you can remember you are primary, and any identity you adopt is secondary. The power is in you.

Practice

Take a moment to think about what masks you've agreed to wear over the years. Do you identify with any particular groups, styles, or philosophies? Whatever identity or identities you may have adopted, remember that you have the power deep down to remove those masks and reveal your true self.

Finding Your Center

Sometimes our lives can become so busy and chaotic it feels as if we were caught in a hurricane. With so many things swirling around us, our stress levels rise as we try to control not only the things we can, but also the peripheral things outside ourselves that we can't. In trying to control the entire swell of the hurricane, we give our power away; the result is suffering.

It's easy to get caught up in the hurricane and forget to stay in our center, in our power. The hurricane exists because you exist. The strength of the hurricane comes directly from you. With awareness, you can get back to your center. You can find the calm in the storm.

Practice

To get back to your center and take back your power, ask yourself: What is the most important thing to me in my life?

Once you know the answer, taming the hurricane becomes much easier. You can better focus on what is most important and stop focusing on all the other stuff. Being aware of what is most important in your life allows you to stay in balance with everything you do.

Fun

Like our professional life, much of our spiritual life is practiced with focus and a serious intention. There is nothing wrong with this, so long as we remember that our lives are not complete without another very important component: having fun!

Taking time to play and laugh can help you relax, ease tension, and stay balanced—all of which are keys to maintaining awareness. If you go too long without some recreation time, you can get caught in a trap of seriousness, which narrows your window of perception and causes you to see everything as either a chore or a challenge instead of an opportunity. Instead of embracing life, it becomes a chore of buckling down to get through the next obstacle, the next meeting, or the next hour.

Bringing some nourishing fun into each day remedies dry, brittle seriousness. Play supercharges your creativity. Fun is not just something we do after the work is done; it's a necessity for health and happiness.

Practice

With awareness, remember that balance is the key to a wonderful life, and fun is an integral component. Take on the serious quest of bringing some fun into this day.

Narrators and Conditional Love

Without awareness, our narrators can play a major role in our romantic relationships by placing conditions and expectations on our partner's behavior. This occurs every time you hear statements in your head such as:

"My partner *should* be doing this."

"Our love is *supposed* to be this way."

"My partner *must change* this for me to be happy."

All of these statements exemplify love with conditions. Our narrators are the source of these kinds of statements, as they continuously promulgate the beliefs and ideas we have agreed with throughout life about how relationships should be.

Practice

When we judge our beloved through the eyes of the narrators, we miss out on the beautiful person he or she is in the present moment. We get lost in our attachment to what our partner should or should not be, rather than loving them unconditionally.

With awareness, accept the people closest to you exactly as they are. When the narrators speak up with criticism or conditions, simply smile and say to yourself, "No, thank you, I no longer agree with your position." Commit to showing those closest to you how much you really love them by treating them kindly no matter what the narrators may say.

Recognizing Self-Domestication

We are the only creatures on this planet that self-domesticate. Any time you create an expectation for yourself that is the condition for your own acceptance and self-love, know that you are self-domesticating, and the tool you use to accomplish this is self-judgment.

Self-judgment is the punishment for not meeting your own expectations—it's how you bully yourself into being the person you think you should be.

Practice

With awareness, notice all the subtle ways in which you judge yourself for failing to meet your own expectations. Noticing them is the first step to releasing them. You are perfect exactly the way you are. There is nothing you need to do to be worthy of your own self-love.

The Importance
of Correct Listening

Listening to what others say without giving their words power over you allows you to become aware of your own truth. It enables you to see what is real versus what is just an illusion, a lie fueled by a sense of personal importance.

If we are coming from a place of awareness, our truth does not need to be defended through the ego-feeding mechanics of an argument. It requires very little energy on our part to simply state our truth, if we choose to state it.

Practice

Today, listen to what others say with an open mind, hearing them completely and honoring their point of view. Be careful not to criticize their words or place them on a pedestal, but rather honor their ideas in the same way that you would hope they honor your own. They decide what is true for them, and you decide what is true for you.

Awareness Can Set You Free

When you are aware, the agreements you make are not subjugated to an identity. But when you are not aware, you are a slave to the identity you have created.

For example, I am free to choose to agree, disagree, scrutinize, and engage with the Toltec philosophy, or any other, as much as I want. I am free to relate to and engage in relationships with people who have preferences for other traditions or philosophies. I am not subject to the identity of "I am a Toltec."

That is true with every belief: You engage it for as long as you want to engage it, knowing full well that you are a living being with the full potential to experience life with or without that agreement.

Practice

To what identities have you subjugated yourself? With awareness, see that the real you is greater than any identity you adopt.

The Five Senses

Our five senses represent five ways to become aware of life. Most of us rely primarily on the gift of sight, but the gifts of hearing, touch, and smell also help you gather data from the world around you. Each of these senses can easily get dulled if you don't consciously use it. To keep them at their brightest, engage with your senses one at a time, being present with each one.

When you slow down and tune in through taste or touch, different aspects of yourself are awakened from the sleep of habit. When you take the time to listen or smell fully, your brain gets excited to experience the sounds or scents of this present moment. When you look with new eyes, everything can be new.

Practice

After reading this, take a few moments to close your eyes and just listen, experiencing the myriad sounds around you. What do you learn about yourself and the world through this window of perception? Paying attention to all five senses helps keep you grounded in awareness.

Breaking Free of Judgment

The fear of unconditionally loving yourself only comes from the conditions you've placed on yourself. Every time you don't live up to your self-imposed conditions, your internal judge says, "I have failed" or "I am not worthy."

These judgments are often reinforced by others who have a need to impose conditions upon us, but their strength only comes from your endorsement of their validity. As your domestication becomes complete, you set up an elaborate internal defense system that self-strengthens by denying the opportunity to even question these negative thoughts.

This is where fear stems from, protecting ourselves from the poison that these judgments give. The good news is that it only requires a single step to begin to break free. As soon as we question our beliefs, the walls of its support begin to collapse.

Practice

To love yourself unconditionally requires but a single step: saying, "Yes! I am worthy of my own love."

True Quality

True quality comes from bringing your full attention to anything that you do and doing your best, whether that be in your professional life, your personal relationships, or your hobbies.

Quality comes from taking the time necessary to learn, understand, and practice the skills needed to do something with excellence. Here, excellence is not the same as perfection through the eyes of the judge, which is the basis for conditional love and is ultimately unachievable. Excellence is simply good work that you are proud of.

Making something of true quality cannot be done without awareness.

Practice

Are there any areas of your life where the quality of your involvement could be improved? This question is not meant to fuel your harsh inner judge, but rather help you notice what areas of your life you can engage in more fully through awareness. When you engage in life with awareness, whatever you do is done with excellence.

Loving Unconditionally

Suffering occurs when we try to fight the evolution of love, when we attempt to negotiate by saying things like, "You should love me like this" or "I should love you like that."

But when you look deep inside yourself, you realize that love is there, that it has always been there, for you and for everyone else, and you can't control it. Why would you want to?

Practice

With awareness, repeat the following statement: "Today I will rest in love and its ever-changing manifestations."

Practicing Nonattachment

When you believe some person, place, thing, or situation must stay in its "rightful" place, exactly as it is, for you to be happy, then you have confused this external thing with who you are. In short, you have created an attachment.

When this external thing changes, and eventually everything does, how will you react? If you have placed your sense of self in it, then you will have to fight for it, you will have to argue for it; in the process, you will create suffering for yourself and those around you.

Practice

Today, remember that you are always you, whole and complete. People, places, and things come and go, but there is nothing outside you that can change your beautiful perfection.

Awareness of the Breath

The breath is the expression of your pure life force, the manifestation of intent. Without breath, life in this body is not possible, yet many people have not taken a conscious breath in a long, long time.

Practice

Stop for just a moment and breathe. Be conscious of the life force as it comes in and out of your body.

At this moment, you are alive and everything is possible. The only thing that matters is that breath. Your internal narrators may speak up and try to tell you that you have more important things to do or think about, but ignore them.

Have faith that all you need to do at this very moment is breathe. Close your eyes and listen to the breath without distractions. Let this remind you that all that matters is happening right now.

Every time you inhale, imagine love going directly to your heart, then circulating throughout your body, cleansing every emotion and every concept in your mind. With each exhale, release any idea or belief that no longer serves your highest good.

Changing Your Mind

Despite the fact that change is a constant in life, one area that many of us have trouble with is allowing ourselves to change our mind.

But as we change, the way we view the world also changes. As a result, some things that we never would have agreed with before, we may now want to say yes to. The opposite is also true, as we may now find ourselves saying no to things we once agreed with.

When this happens, our internal narrators will often speak up and yell, "No! This is not who you are. You've never done that before!" This is the voice of the ego, which holds on to the past and control. Oftentimes our opinions and agreements from the past are based on other people's ideas rather than our own.

The willingness to change your mind is a sign of maturity. It shows you are growing up and thinking for yourself.

Practice

With awareness, look back over the areas where you have changed your mind in your life. These are often points of growth—more reason to continually evaluate your beliefs and change your mind about any that are no longer serving you.

Thinking in the Affirmative

Starting a new practice that can silence your inner critic and create lasting awareness takes time. Those negative inner thoughts didn't develop overnight, and they won't disappear overnight, either. But know that this is one of, if not *the,* most important things you will ever do. Begin with knowing that you are enough. Today, I ask you to honor and love yourself just because you are.

Practice

Say to yourself right now, "My life is worth something." With that statement, you plant the seed of unconditional love in your heart and mind as you shine a light on the darkness of conditional love.

Repeating this simple affirmation regularly creates a practice that overtakes the negative voices of your internal narrators, the ones that say, "You are no good" or "You are not worthy" or "You are not enough."

The truth is that you are more than enough! Perfect, exactly the way you are!

Death

In the Toltec tradition, we have a practice that helps us increase our awareness of the beauty of life by befriending an unlikely ally: death.

Imagine what would happen if you stopped living as if you will be around forever, and you embraced the truth that each day is a gift beyond measure. The angel of death can come for you at any moment.

When you are aware of your own mortality—not as something to fear, but as a friend and teacher—every moment becomes crisp and perfect just as it is. Colors are richer, friendships are more precious, and problems lose their hold on you. It becomes more important to joyfully wring every drop out of each day than to worry about what was or what might have been.

Practice

Pose this question to yourself: "If today were the last day of my life, how would I treat myself and others? What conversations would I have that I've been putting off? What would I choose to enjoy today?"

War and Peace

The eyes of the judge, the parasite, the internal narrators, the mitote, the Smokey Mirror, domestication—these are all metaphors from the Toltec tradition that explain the workings of your mind. The mind has created an egoic identity based on concepts of scarcity, judgment, and competition that it has difficulty letting go of. But the only place war can occur in you is in your mind.

The real you is pure bliss and always at peace. That's why I say that every person I meet, every person I see, is an expression of the Authentic Self. It's only our thoughts and our judgments that keep us from seeing this truth about ourselves and others, a truth so simple that it's sometimes difficult for the mind to grasp.

Practice

Sit in the present moment and let everything be as it is. You, I, and everything around you are perfect. Let the perfection be.

Conclusion

Although you have come to the end of this journey of daily meditations, the practice of awareness is a lifelong adventure.

As you go out into the world each day, the Dream of the Planet challenges you to maintain your awareness as you reengage in life, navigating the illusions of domestication and conditional love that are expressed so frequently in our society.

Most people do not live in a cloistered monastery in the middle of nowhere, free to practice awareness in solitude. They, like you, live in a community—in the Dream of the Planet—where the people they love and the noise of the world attempt to hook their attention in every possible way. Even those who do live in an ashram or a monastery, a space created almost exclusively for practicing awareness, will tell you that their world is far from being distraction-free. So, regardless of where you are, coming into and out of awareness is a universal human condition.

For myself, I enter the world each day knowing that I may lose my awareness and temporarily fall back into the habits of domestication and conditional love. The people I interact with put forth an expectation of who I'm supposed to be and how I'm supposed to behave, and if I begin to believe in their expectations—even a little—I've subjugated myself to their idea of perfection. That is the temptation conditional love presents for us all.

For those of us on the Toltec path, or really any other spiritual path for that matter, we must be equally careful not to turn our pursuit of personal freedom or any other method of self-improvement into a new form of self-domestication and model for conditional self-love: "If I don't live up to my expectations, then I am not worthy of my own love." Practicing awareness can help stop us from falling into this trap.

Here's a personal story that illustrates this ongoing challenge quite well. In January, I looked at myself and said, "Miguel, you are perfect, and I love you exactly the way you are—and I think you would be healthier and enjoy your life even more if you got back into running."

In years past, I had run quite regularly, but I had not done so in some time. Consequently, I dusted off my old sneakers and went for a run. I made it two-thirds of a mile before I had to stop. I could feel my heart pounding, and it took me some time to catch my breath. I was surprised at how difficult it was for me to make it just that far.

At that moment I had a choice: I could call myself a "lazy bum" and judge myself accordingly, or I could realize that this was just my starting point: "Be gentle with yourself, Miguel. This is where you are today, and you are perfect exactly as you are." My goal, with practice, was to be able to run five miles without stopping by the end of May.

So, without any domestication or conditional love, I began my running routine. Before the end of April, I'd met my goal! I was enjoying myself very much. But like any person who gets wrapped up in work, family, and life, I got distracted, and my running routine fell to the wayside.

When I was able to start running again a few weeks later, I expected to be able to run five miles without stopping, as that was the mark of my recent achievement. But I could only run two! At that moment, the disappointment seeped in, and I could hear the voice of my internal judge yelling, "What is the matter with you?! How are you not able to still run five miles?"

My mind immediately blamed external circumstances and other people for this, then I watched as I got angry with myself for not keeping up with my own benchmark. Self-judgment in the form of "you lazy bum!" filled my mind. Upon hearing my narrators say this, my awareness kicked back in, and I realized the old ways of self-domestication were attempting to regain their foothold, this time with new conditions.

Had I continued on this road of self-judgment, I would have placed my "Miguel, the good runner" persona on a pedestal, making it a new model for self-domestication. From this point of view, I would need to run five miles just to consider myself acceptable, and I wouldn't consider myself perfect as I worked toward that goal. As a result, my motivation would become corrupted, as I turned the noble idea of getting healthier via running into a new form of self-domestication.

As with all pursuits of perfection that are undertaken with this motivation, the ego is never satisfied for very long. If I were to hit five miles, pretty soon that would not be enough. Next would be eight miles, then ten, and before long, I would need to run a marathon to truly be perfect!

Every time we use domestication and conditional love as a motivator for change rather than unconditional self-love, suffering is inevitable.

This example shows us how subtly the habits of self-judgment and self-domestication can hook us. Without awareness, we unconsciously create the expectations of who we think we are supposed to be based on the agreements we have made in the Dream of the Planet. For any expectation that goes unmet, we judge ourselves accordingly.

To be clear, there is nothing wrong with having goals; they are motivators, or focal points, for us to create the existence we desire. The problem lies in the fact that we use goals as a reason to either love ourselves or reject ourselves, corrupting them into instruments for conditional love. Thus, our happiness relies on our "success," and because this type of success mainly exists in the future and is rarely, if ever, achieved, we are never able to enjoy who we are at this very moment. We spend so much time looking ahead and waiting for happiness to come that we forget to look around and enjoy who we are right now. If we do manage to achieve momentary success by this standard, we live with the constant fear of losing it.

Self-judgment is the root of our suffering. When we self-judge, we aren't able to see and enjoy who we really are at this very moment, because we are constantly evaluating ourselves by an illusory standard set by our own agreements. We have been conditioned to believe that our self-acceptance relies on our accomplishments.

When we reach our goals, our self-esteem rises; when we don't, we think less of ourselves. This is how the great majority of people interact with one another, imposing beliefs onto one another and subjugating themselves to the judgment of others. This is how the illusion of conditional love spreads throughout the Dream of the Planet. When we judge another, we are punishing that person for agreements they never made. Through our judgment, we try to force them to make the agreement we want them to make, thus imposing our beliefs on them.

How can we stop judging ourselves and others? By accepting ourselves just the way we are right now. Once we accept ourselves completely, we will stop judging others. You cannot give to others what you have not given to yourself.

It is through the practice of awareness that we are able to see the perfection that exists in others and ourselves.

Most of us have experienced incredible periods of awareness in which we are totally in the moment, going with the flow of life. But sadly, these experiences are often short-lived. One of the most difficult tasks we'll ever be faced with is staying in our awareness.

For example, one day you have a moment of clarity: You see what you have created for yourself through domestication and conditional love, and you express a decision to shift the way you live your life. You begin a long progress of reestablishing a communion with yourself by creating harmony in your Personal Dream.

You combine personal experiences along your journey with your mind's understanding of how to manifest awareness. You see the mechanism of conditional love and how it is causing suffering in your life and the lives of others, and you begin to let go with compassion and forgiveness. The seed of unconditional love sprouts in your heart and blossoms as you say to yourself, "I am worthy of my own love simply because I am alive." Your Personal Dream begins to move with the harmony of unconditional love.

Then, as you get distracted by everyday life, you begin to forget this new perspective and your focus slips from your Personal Dream to the Dream of the Planet. Your harmony is shaken as you give in to the illusion. But before long, you have another moment of clarity, and you start the process again—this time with a little more resolve and a little more experience.

This is the normal course of events for most of us, and we must remember that practice makes the master.

By practicing awareness, we create harmony in our Personal Dream by stopping the downward spiral of domestication and conditional love. We see the chasm in the choice between loving others with conditional love versus unconditional love. Through practice, we learn to dance all over again with compassion. We develop the ability to respect others' creations and understand that they can only relate to us based on their own perception, which is set by their own levels of attachment. We also develop the ability to have compassion and respect for ourselves in our interactions with others.

Through awareness, we realize that our "no" is just as powerful as our "yes." We do not allow our intent to be subjugated by the internal judge, nor do we give in to the need of another who wants us to subjugate ourselves to his or her intent. We begin to share our unconditional love with our community with the understanding that we are responsible only for our intent, not the intent of others. We are equals in the creation of the Dream of Us.

In the Toltec tradition, *controlled folly* is the art of staying in our awareness of self as we engage the illusion of the Dream of the Planet.

We remain in our awareness by practicing compassion and respect as an act of unconditional love for self and others. It is the art of controlled folly that allows us to continue to live in an environment where the noise of life can pull us in every direction. This art is the mastery of living in the Dream of the Planet while still practicing awareness in everyday life. Like a stone that has been submerged in water for years yet internally it remains dry, controlled folly is being a part of the ecosystem without letting its surroundings seep in.

Who I am right now is perfect! Why? Simply because I exist at this very moment of life. Regardless of whether I am able to run two miles, two-thirds of a mile, or not at all, I enjoy who I am simply because I exist. If I choose to run five miles or even participate in a marathon, I am doing so because I *want to* not because I *have to*. Whether or not I succeed at any goal I set for myself, I am still happy being me while doing my best to follow through with my intention.

Living a life of awareness is knowing that you always have a choice in how you express your intent—that in any single moment you can pivot and shift with faith in yourself as an expression of love. You can engage awareness through any beautiful tradition that exists in the world and put your awareness into practice with the tradition that resonates with you.

Toltec is a Nahuatl word that means "artist." The whole world is full of artists in every tradition. We make those traditions vibrate with life by our intent. Let your heart express itself in the language it knows; let it dance with the song that carries the rhythm of your heart; and let love be expressed through every part of your body. You are the artist who knows how to express this love to the world. The world is your blank canvas, and your intent is the instrument with which you will make your great masterpiece, an ever-evolving expression of love.

"Living a life of awareness" is an idea, a symbol that helps us focus our intent to create a life in which we enjoy being who we are and being with the people we love, creating together the Dream of Us in harmony, respect, and compassion. This is the expression of unconditional love. Love is the perfect balance of generosity and gratitude, and through awareness you can choose to live in this harmony.

Acknowledgments

With all of my love, I honor my teachers, Madre Sarita and don Miguel Ruiz, and my brother who shares this tradition with me lovingly, don Jose Ruiz. To my beautiful wife, Susan, my wonderful children, Alejandro and Audrey, mi mamá, Coco, my brother, Leo, my Mama Gaya, my sisters, Jules, Jennifer, and Kimberly-Jeanne, and my brother Ramakrishna (Trey), thank you for your wisdom and love that we share with one another. I love you.

I want to express my gratitude to Randy Davila, whose love and passion have helped me share my family's oral tradition by being the publisher of my books. To Allison Jacob, HeatherAsh Amara, Janet Mills, Carol Killman Rosenberg, Kristie Macris, Susie Pitzen, Adrian Morgan, Jane Hagaman, Tania Seymour, Be Engler, Jill Mangino, and everyone at Hierophant Publishing who helped me manifest this wonderful book, thank you for all your hard work and incredible contribution of your talents to give this book life.

Thank you to the Creator for the inspiration that fills these pages with love.

About the Author

At the age of fourteen, don Miguel Ruiz Jr. apprenticed to his father don Miguel and his grandmother Madre Sarita. From that early age, he was called upon to translate Madre Sarita's prayers, lectures, and workshops from Spanish into English. In this way, through constant repetition and review, he learned the content of her teachings in both languages. Through interpreting for Madre Sarita, don Miguel Jr. came to understand the power of faith. He saw firsthand how his grandmother manifested her intent to heal people, both physically and spiritually.

Don Miguel Jr.'s apprenticeship lasted ten years. When he reached his mid-twenties, his father intensified his training. At the apex of this power journey, don Miguel said to his eldest son, "Find your way out. Go home and master death by becoming alive."

For the past six years, don Miguel Jr. has applied the lessons learned from his father and grandmother to define and enjoy his own personal freedom while achieving peace with all of creation. Being able to apply his teachings to the world around him gave Miguel Jr. a new understanding of the lessons his father and grandmother had passed on to him, once again giving him the desire to pass on his tradition. After decades of training, Miguel Jr. was finally ready to share everything he had learned. As a *nagual* in the Toltec tradition, he now helps others discover optimal physical and spiritual health, so that they may achieve their own personal freedom.

Don Miguel Jr. is married and has two young children.

www.miguelruizjr.com

Hierophant Publishing
8301 Broadway, Suite 219
San Antonio, TX 78209
888-800-4240

www.hierophantpublishing.com